Changing Public and Private Roles in Agricultural Service Provision

Diana Carney

Changing Public and Private Roles in Agricultural Service Provision

Diana Carney

Overseas Development Institute

Natural Resources Group

A CIP Publications data record may be obtained from the British Library

ISBN 0 85003 347 8

© Overseas Development Institute 1998

Published by the Overseas Development Institute
Portland House, Stag Place
London SW1E 5DP

All rights reserved. No part of this may be reproduced by any means, nor transmitted, nor stored electronically, without the written permission of the publisher.

Printed by The Chameleon Press Ltd, London

Contents

Preface   vii

Acknowledgements   viii

1. Introduction   1
   1.1 New goals   2
      1.1.1 Improving institutional accountability   2
      1.1.2 Improving effectiveness   3
      1.1.3 Improving efficiency   4
   1.2 Framework for analysis   5
   1.3 Relationships between goods and services   7

2. Fertiliser supply   9
   2.1 Changes in supply or supplier   9
   2.2 Economic analysis   10
   2.3 Progress towards new goals   12
   2.4 Focus on the rural poor   12
   2.5 Lessons   14

3. Seed supply   16
   3.1 Changes in supply or supplier   16
   3.2 Economic analysis   21
   3.3 Progress towards new goals   23
   3.4 Focus on the rural poor   25
   3.5 Lessons   26

4. Agricultural research systems   28
   4.1 Changes in supply or supplier   28
   4.2 Economic analysis   30
   4.3 Progress towards new goals   32
   4.4 Focus on the rural poor   35
   4.5 Lessons   37

5. Agricultural extension systems   39
   5.1 Changes in supply or supplier   39
   5.2 Economic analysis   44
   5.3 Progress towards new goals   46
   5.4 Focus on the rural poor   48
   5.5 Lessons   50

6. Veterinary services ... 52
   6.1 Changes in supply or supplier ... 52
   6.2 Economic analysis ... 53
   6.3 Progress towards new goals ... 56
   6.4 Focus on the rural poor ... 58
   6.5 Lessons ... 59

7. Rural credit ... 61
   7.1 Changes in supply or supplier ... 61
   7.2 Economic analysis ... 62
   7.3 Progress towards new goals ... 64
   7.4 Focus on the rural poor ... 65
   7.5 Lessons ... 66

8. Agricultural produce marketing ... 68
   8.1 Changes in supply or supplier ... 68
   8.2 Economic analysis ... 69
   8.3 Progress towards new goals ... 70
   8.4 Focus on the rural poor ... 71
   8.5 Lessons ... 72

9. Conclusion ... 74

Bibliography ... 81

Preface

This review was originally undertaken as part of the DFID- (then ODA-) funded Rural Resources and Poverty Research Programme (1993–6). The programme focused on the changing role of the state in natural resources management and the provision of supporting rural services. The objective was to derive policy guidelines about:

- how to identify those areas of management and service provision for which the state should retain responsibility

- which other potential providers are best suited to take over responsibilities ceded by governments

- how to manage the process of change

- how the role of the state must evolve so that those activities which it does still undertake are performed with the greatest effectiveness, in terms of meeting the needs of the rural poor (while not unduly compromising other valid objectives, such as increasing overall production or maintaining biodiversity).

A number of subject areas were covered, namely: agricultural services (including research and extension), forestry, water resources and pastoralism. Literature reviews were completed and fieldwork was conducted in Africa, Asia and Latin America. The main findings of the project are reported in detail elsewhere (Carney and Farrington, 1998).

This review was conducted at a reasonably early stage in the project and published as an ODI Working Paper (no. 81) in 1995. The current version has been substantially updated and draws on work done in the context of other research projects (largely financed by DFID). In particular, the author has recently produced a series of 'Key Sheets' which are designed to assist DFID with decision-making about its involvement in resource management and rural service provision. These sheets aim to distil field experience and theoretical debate and to provide readers with an easy and up-to-date point of reference on issues relating to development in the natural environment. Elements of these Key Sheets are included in this revised literature review. The revised review also takes into account the recent move, on the part of both DFID and the World Bank (amongst others), to supporting rural livelihoods as a whole, rather than focusing on narrow sub-sectors (such as agricultural research or extension). Although the review is structured around the traditional sub-sectors efforts are made to demonstrate the links between these; a new section on these links has been incorporated.

Acknowledgements

The publication and distribution of this review has been financed by the Department for International Development. This support is gratefully acknowledged. However, the opinions expressed are those of the author and do not necessarily reflect those of the Department for International Development.

Thanks are also extended to Adrienne Watson at ODI for her work on formatting and setting the text both for the original Working Paper and this updated version.

1. Introduction

Following independence most developing countries chose to follow 'statist' models of development whereby the public sector controlled all key aspects of the economy. In the agricultural sector this included government dominating or monopolising the supply of physical inputs, credit provision, research, extension and marketing systems, either directly or through specially established agricultural parastatals. However, financial crises and extremely poor progress in raising economic and social well-being in many countries have led to a fundamental rethinking of the role of government since the early 1980s (World Bank, 1981; Gros, 1994).

The concepts which now dominate the debate surrounding the role of the state in rural development are effectiveness, efficiency and accountability. All three are related as will be outlined below, but it is important at the outset to clarify the way in which each is used in this review. *Effectiveness* refers to the ability to meet goals, objectives or needs – here these are the goals, needs and objectives of the rural population. *Efficiency* refers to the way in which goals are met – it implies that this is done at as low a cost as is possible without having a negative impact. *Accountability* is institutionalised responsiveness to those who are affected by one's actions. Thus accountability contributes to effectiveness and only institutions which are effective can be classified as truly efficient. In a sense, then, efficiency subsumes the other goals.

The complication is that efficiency, as defined above, does not always coincide exactly with *economic efficiency*. In general, economic or Pareto efficiency is achieved when nobody can be made better off without somebody else being made worse off. In the absence of market failures, markets are considered to be the best allocative mechanism for achieving this. However, if governments wish to service the needs of those sections of the population with inadequate purchasing power which are not served by markets, they will need to intervene in pure market allocations. This does not imply that they entirely sweep aside such allocations, but rather that they supplement them in particular areas. According to the definition above they can do so and still be efficient (so long as they adopt the least cost method of doing so), which would not necessarily be true given a narrowly economic definition of efficiency. Such efficiency might thus be thought of as '*social efficiency*'. This is not, however, an easy concept with which to work since it has no natural boundaries. To the extent that it involves meeting people's needs there must always be an additional decision taken about how far the public sector should go in doing this, given scarce resources and inevitable trade-offs between provision in different areas.

After looking at the goals of reform and laying out the framework for analysis this paper analyses each of the major categories of agricultural goods and services in turn:

fertiliser supply, seed supply, agricultural research systems, agricultural extension systems, veterinary services, rural financial services and agricultural produce marketing services. Examples of changes in supply or supplier are taken from the literature and the economic characteristics of the goods in question are reviewed. The effect of change upon the rural poor is particularly highlighted as are overall improvements in effectiveness in the provision of the goods in question. Lastly, general guidelines for the future are drawn out of the foregoing analysis.

1.1 New goals

It is widely held that guidelines as to the areas from which governments should retreat and those where it should maintain a role are best drawn from the market. In general, public sector intervention in those areas of the market which do function is not considered efficient and the view is that it should therefore be avoided whenever possible (Smith and Thomson, 1991). Exceptions should only be made in areas where market failures occur or to which markets do not extend.

The first step towards achieving economic efficiency is therefore to remove any macroeconomic distortions, which will in turn reduce the incidence of market failure and thence the need for government intervention. This has been the main goal of the economic reform programmes imposed as part of structural adjustment loans (World Bank, 1981). Such programmes have, however, been criticised for their rigidity and over zealous cost-cutting which has sometimes left less well-off groups without the basic social and economic infrastructure they require. Poorer groups living in remote areas tend to be ill-served by markets, because they do not have sufficient purchasing power to be attractive to profit-oriented companies, especially given their very complex needs and the high costs associated with reaching them. It is these groups which are most likely to remain dependent upon government, or at least non-commercial suppliers, in the long term.

Recognition of the continued needs of such people has recently led to a far greater emphasis being placed upon the development of partnerships between the public and the private (often private non-commercial e.g. NGO) sectors in poorer areas. The role that the public sector can, or should be able to, play in facilitating the private sector and stimulating the development of new types of relationships and market-based contracts has been recognised. While at one stage it might have appeared contradictory, it is now quite uncontroversial to suggest that 'for free markets to work better, the government must also work better' (Klitgaard, 1991) and that 'market-orientation and state minimalism, far from going together, are incompatible' (Streeten, 1996).

1.1.1 Improving institutional accountability

Accountability is very much part of the fabric of competitive markets, and increased accountability is one route to enhanced effectiveness, as noted above. In principle, when consumers pay for goods they can use their purchasing power both to express and to enforce the satisfaction of their needs (although this does assume that consumers are almost fully informed about their options) (Antholt, 1991; Merrill Sands and Collion, 1993).

In areas where governments continue to play a key role, however, increased accountability will have to be deliberately pursued. For the value of accountability lies not only in its contribution to effectiveness and efficiency, but also in the role it plays in strengthening civil society. (This is the rationale behind many donor- and NGO-sponsored village-level capacity building projects. See, for example, Mosse, 1996). Public sector cost recovery schemes can contribute to accountability. They certainly increase user ownership of and interest in delivery systems. However, unless clients have viable alternative sources of supply they can only withdraw their contributions as a last resort which makes such schemes somewhat imperfect. Other ways of improving the accountability of public services include opening up communication links between clients (the rural people) and the public sector (for example forums for consultation preferably with some resources to allocate) and putting in place an incentive structure within the public sector which evaluates and rewards individuals according to their success in meeting the needs of the client.

1.1.2 Improving effectiveness

Donors and various types of groups within developing countries (such as farmers' organisations, grass roots movements, agricultural development foundations and non-governmental organisations) have been particularly critical of governments' poor records in meeting the needs of the rural population. In some cases governments have recognised their failings independently. Impending elections, for example in Tanzania, or the fear of unrest, for example in Indonesia, have also contributed to the pressure for change. Whatever the cause of the new awareness, the result is the same; public sector institutions throughout the world have begun to change, some already quite profoundly.

In the past government monopolies were insulated from public pressure and research organisations were isolated from their clients (Antholt, 1994; Sims and Leonard, 1990; Merrill Sands and Collion, 1993). Extension workers 'transferred' inappropriate technologies (Okali et al., 1994; Röling, 1990; de Coninck and Tinguiri, 1992) and inputs failed to arrive in time to fit in with the agricultural calendar (Sims and Leonard, 1990). Marketing boards were seen by donors as a particular problem. They were frequently wasteful, corrupt and unresponsive to changes in supply. They provided neither adequate price incentives to farmers nor – in many cases – viable purchasing structures (World Bank, 1994).

However, the problem was not simply the potential for abuse inherent in the monopoly situation, but also a fundamental lack of concern on behalf of governments, individuals within governments and donors for rural producers. At best they were treated as ignorant and in need of modernisation and at worst they were actively exploited by urban elites in search of cheap food (Schiff and Valdés, 1992; Bates, 1981; Jaeger, 1992). Consequently public sector institutions in many countries made insufficient effort to identify and service their needs. The pressure for this to change and for the client (the farmer or the rural dweller more generally) to be placed firmly at the centre of an integrated system of rural service provision in the interests of overall livelihood enhancement has now become enormous, for it is recognised that only in this way will rural people be in a position to fulfil their true potential (Kaimowitz, 1990; Röling, 1990; Röling, 1991).

Nevertheless, the task of identifying and serving the needs of rural people in general, and the poorest who are ill-served by markets in particular, remains daunting. The diversity and complexity of rural livelihoods means that efforts to alleviate poverty in rural areas will have to be multi-faceted and holistic. For example, many of the poorest are landless and will not therefore be reached through traditional agricultural interventions; other methods of assessing their needs and supporting them in a demand-led process of development must be found. The challenge is for government institutions to adapt as fast as the environment in which they are working. One way for them to do this is to seek more responsive institutional structures through decentralisation and deconcentration and to form partnerships with other actors who have a better record of success in this area (for example, some NGOs and rural people's organisations).

In many areas private sector institutions, be they private companies, non-profit organisations or groups of individuals with a direct stake in the good in question (e.g. farmers' organisations) will be the most effective providers of goods and services. Their links with consumers, either through market mechanisms or their use of participatory planning techniques, tend to be stronger. If the public sector focuses on identifying the core areas which are not serviced by such actors and the areas in which such actors might play a role but only with some government assistance, it can then concentrate its remaining resources and efforts on a smaller number of issues. Although there is no guarantee that it will be more effective in these remaining core areas, its chances of being so should be enhanced.

1.1.3 Improving efficiency

For governments there are two main aspects to improving efficiency. The first relates to their role as 'manager' of the markets which contribute to overall system efficiency. The public sector should withdraw from areas where markets function and instead invest in the infrastructure which makes markets possible and extends them to poorer areas. This may be either physical, for example roads, or more institutional, for example regulatory mechanisms to reduce consumer risk, well-enforced contract law and better channels for information dissemination.

The second relates to governments' own operations in areas of legitimate involvement and the need to cut costs. Many reforms originated from an absolute need to reduce the financial burden on the state. Donors highlighted many areas of very wasteful expenditure which have been the first targets for reform. In particular, pressure to cut public sector staff numbers has been great since salaries have accounted for an enormous proportion of domestic spending (Antholt, 1994; Nunberg and Nellis, 1990; World Bank, 1994a).

However, it is also becoming increasingly apparent that indiscriminate cost cutting, without regard to the effectiveness of services, is counter-productive in the long term. A more profitable approach is to look for cheaper ways of doing things, for example through: forming alliances with other non-profit organisations in areas where the private sector does not reach; increasing the use of mass media in extension; establishing 'matching funds' at community level; and putting in place cost recovery schemes in areas which can bear part, but not all, of the cost of provision of goods and services. The sections relating to individual resources highlight efforts made to date.

1.2 Framework for analysis

There has been much analysis of the impacts of structural adjustment and reform programmes upon macroeconomic indicators, such as growth, and social indicators, such as life expectancy and infant mortality. There have been far fewer accounts, however, of the day-to-day effects of changes in terms of access by rural people to the goods and services which they require to sustain their livelihoods. Most commentators have looked at farmers' responses to price incentives and the reduction of subsidies rather than the mechanics of how the new supply systems function and whom they serve. And until quite recently there has been relatively little attention devoted to the ways in which governments' activities have changed rather than simply diminished. This omission is now being rectified as new partnerships develop and new thinking about the role of government permeates more deeply (Carney and Farrington, 1998).

The most developed area in the literature remains that which deals with the economic characteristics of the goods and services in question (Smith and Thomson, 1991; Umali, Feder and de Haan, 1992; Umali and Schwartz, 1994; Schwartz, 1994; World Bank, 1993). The classification of goods according to the principles of traditional welfare economics and the analysis of market imperfections help to indicate where continuing government involvement is likely to be necessary.

The common framework is to classify goods according to the degree to which they exhibit the two key properties of excludability (those who have not paid for a good are excluded from consuming it) and subtractability (one person's consumption of the goods reduces its availability to others). In general only those goods which are both highly excludable and highly subtractable (private goods) are candidates for private supply (see Table 1). If the supply of other types of goods is left entirely to market mechanisms, the result will be undersupply and a loss of economic efficiency. Since the marginal social cost of adding a new user is zero it does not make to sense to set prices which will exclude anyone. If, conversely, private goods are subsidised then they tend to be used at levels higher than the economic optimum. Costs will exceed

Table 1: Economic characteristics

Type of good	Subtractability	Excludability
Private good	✓	✓
Public good	X	X
Toll good	X	✓
Common pool good	✓	X

benefits and other criteria for limiting supply will have to be introduced; experience has shown that these are often arbitrarily defined.

The concepts are common to all the literature although the terminology varies slightly. Characterisations are as shown in Table 1 (after Umali and Schwartz, 1994). It should, however, be noted that characterisations based upon welfare economics do not generate immutable laws about supply, as will become apparent in the sections relating to particular goods and services. The prevalence of incomplete or imperfect markets and distortions in almost all areas of economic activity, particularly in developing countries and particularly in the agricultural sector, often makes theory a poor guide to practice. Thus, under certain circumstances private commercial companies *may* choose to supply public, toll or common pool goods. The point is that they generally will not.

Government (or other) intervention is also required in the presence of market failures, including: externalities (either positive or negative) when one individual's consumption of goods automatically affects others; risk and imperfect markets; imperfect information (including incidences of adverse selection or moral hazard when buyers and sellers have differential access to information); and increasing returns to scale (Smith and Thomson, 1991).

Both Smith and Thomson (1991) and Umali and Schwartz (1994) disaggregate the flow of goods and services into provision, financing and regulation as well as consumption. This increases the sophistication of their analysis under conditions of market failure. Both sets of authors argue that while government or another collectivity may be required to intervene in any particular sub-sector, the intervention may be selective, that is it may be limited to one or more of these four constituent activities. Thus, instead of choosing physically to supply a good itself, the public sector could, for example, simply fund private sector provision at optimum levels. In doing this, the state should seek to incorporate private sector practices, such as contracting, creating cost centres etc. into its own activities (ODA, 1994; Hubbard and Smith, 1996). This will facilitate both transparency and economic efficiency as it will directly contribute to reducing the costs of public sector intervention (while also raising the quality of public services).

This disaggregation of goods and services allows for clearer and more accurate interventions by the public sector or others. In other respects, though, it goes against the grain of current thinking on rural livelihoods which urges us to take a more holistic view of needs. Röling (1990) argues that the Agriculture Technology System (ATS), which comprises all the individuals and organisations working on the development, diffusion and use of new and existing technologies in a given geographic area, and the relations among them, should be viewed and analysed as a whole. Likewise, there is an increasing recognition that donors should seek to understand and improve livelihoods as a whole, rather than focusing on particular sub-sectors. This makes for development interventions which are more closely aligned with the complex and shifting nature of life and hence more likely to achieve results in the long term.

This contradiction is more apparent than real. The important step lies in the process of re-aggregation and the recognition of the links between all the various activities involved in supplying goods and services and all the various elements which combine to contribute to sustainable rural livelihoods. These links are of paramount importance. Nevertheless, for the purposes of analytical clarity the following sections take each of the key goods and services in turn. The literature relating to each item is grouped according to:

1) examples of changes in supply or supplier (pulling out any trends and division of responsibilities, e.g. funding/provision)
2) economic analysis of the goods in question using the terminology outlined above
3) evidence (if any) of progress towards meeting the new goals of improved accountability, effectiveness and efficiency
4) focus on evidence (if any) of effects on the rural poor
5) lessons which can be learned from changes to date.

The links between the different goods and services are made apparent throughout the text. However, we conclude this introduction with a brief synthesis of key relationships between the different elements.

1.3 Relationships between goods and services

The topics addressed in the subsequent chapters of this book are linked in their relationships to rural livelihoods. Farmers require a range of goods and services in order to secure their livelihoods. Donor or domestic government intervention in one area must therefore take into consideration prevailing conditions in a number of other areas. Sometimes it may be appropriate to delay intervention in any particular area until these conditions have improved or been altered. Table 2 provides a summary of key relationships between the issues addressed in this review. Brackets indicate a moderate level of interdependence.

Finally, it should be noted that most rural people depend upon multiple sources of income, ranging from petty trade to primary production, remittances to casual employment. It is wrong to conceive of rural people as being exclusively dependent upon agriculture or natural resources more generally. Certainly these might provide the basis for their survival but it may well be that the best prospects for significant livelihood *improvement* lie outside the natural resources sector in the generation of off-farm income. It is beyond the scope of this review to consider essential non-agricultural goods and services though frequent mention is made of the importance to rural people of the maintenance of basic infrastructure (road and communications). The omission of wider discussion of off-farm activities should not be taken as an indication of their lack of importance.

Table 2: Interdependence between topics addressed in this review

Efficient functioning of ↓ Depends upon →	*Agricultural Research*	*Agricultural Extension*	*Seed Supply*	*Rural Finance*	*Livestock Services*	*Fertiliser Supply*	*Agricultural Marketing*
Agricultural Research	■	x	x	(x)			x
Agricultural Extension	x	■	(x)	(x)			x
Seed Supply	x	(x)	■	x		(x)	x
Rural Finance		(x)	(x)	■	(x)	(x)	x
Livestock Services	x	(x)		(x)	■		x
Fertiliser Supply	x	x	x	x		■	x
Agricultural Marketing	(x)	(x)	x	(x)	(x)		■

2. Fertiliser supply

2.1 Changes in supply or supplier

Developing country governments have traditionally exerted monopoly control over agricultural input supplies. Access to (chemical) fertiliser, in particular, has been considered critical to the success of agricultural modernisation and the achievement of increases in production. Governments have thus chosen to manage supplies, directly or through government-sponsored cooperatives, and in many countries to subsidise the price paid by farmers. Funding and production (in this case supply) have gone hand in hand so that where subsidies are in place these are administered through public sector institutions. In many cases the public sector supply systems have been shored up by donors which have been the major financiers of fertiliser imports (and initial sponsors of universal fertiliser subsidies). These donors have often compounded existing problems by supplying fertiliser types unsuitable to local conditions on an irregular and unpredictable basis.

Public sector control, with its attendant isolation from farmers' needs and bureaucratic inefficiencies, has resulted in extremely erratic and untimely supplies. Governments have been unable to provide fertiliser due to shortages in foreign exchange (most developing countries import fertiliser) and limited amounts of money available to finance the subsidies. That fertiliser which has become available has usually ended up in the hands of influential richer farmers (World Bank, 1994a). For this and other reasons, most small farmers continue to use no chemical fertilisers, especially in Africa.

The World Bank (1994a) lists twenty-two African countries which, pre-reform, had both controlled markets and subsidised prices for fertiliser. Removing these subsidies and liberalising markets were easily identifiable goals for early structural adjustment loans and by late 1992 only two of these twenty two countries were recorded as having achieved neither. Fourteen were judged to have succeeded in both while six of the original twenty two retained some price controls.

The progress of such reforms has seldom been smooth. Both Malawi and Nigeria reduced subsidies only to raise them again either explicitly, in the case of Malawi, or in Nigeria by failing to adjust the price of imported fertiliser following devaluation (World Bank, 1994a). Other countries, such as Kenya and Tanzania, were recorded as having liberalised markets but the reality was that public sector institutions still continued to dominate supply – especially on the importing and wholesale side (Mans, 1994; Swamy, 1994).

Clearly, though, there is now greater scope for the private sector and farmers' organisations to become involved in fertiliser supply. Retail distribution tends to entail lower risk and hence be more attractive to the private sector than wholesale supply. Mans (1994) reported that by the beginning of the 1990s about 50% (by volume) of Tanzania's retail fertiliser was in private hands. Following reform and decontrol of prices in Kenya the number of retail outlets in interior locations there has increased, although Swamy (1994) notes that over the period of Kenya's reform estimated fertiliser use declined.

In some countries, such as Senegal, cooperatives stepped in when the government pulled out of supply. While cooperatives can play an important part, especially in remote areas which are ill-served by the private sector, Shepherd argues that they may suffer from many of the same inefficiencies as the government itself (Shepherd, 1989). Many farmers' organisations have also focused on supplying inputs to their members. Bratton and Bingen (1994) argue that the farmers' organisations will tend to focus on the direct provision of goods and services to members rather than aiming to influence broader agricultural or technology policy. Providing concrete services is relatively simple and more readily appreciated by farmers, hence it builds the status and support of the organisation.

2.2 Economic analysis

Of all the agricultural inputs and services under discussion, fertiliser perhaps comes closest to being a pure private good. It is both subtractable and excludable and farmers have almost always paid at least something for its use. As such it is an obvious candidate for private supply, a fact which has not gone unrecognised by donors.

However, there are some complications. Governments which subsidise fertiliser prices and control supply justify their actions in terms of raising aggregate domestic food production and thereby benefiting the nation as a whole. They receive support for this from Fontaine and Sindzingre (1991) who note that the price elasticity of demand for fertiliser is relatively high, implying that small changes in price can have a significant effect on demand. Assuming that output does increase when fertiliser is applied, fertiliser price rises will therefore reduce output, unless organic substitutes which are equally effective can be identified and their use encouraged.

Concern for domestic food supply is common to governments throughout the world. Some respond by subsidising inputs such as fertiliser and others by supporting producer prices; either choice implies intervention in the functionings of the market (Fontaine and Sindzingre, 1991). The issue is likely to be particularly prominent in food deficit countries, especially where imports are constrained by lack of foreign exchange. It is precisely in these countries, however, that fertiliser use should be economically attractive to farmers – so long as two conditions are met. The first is that some proportion of farmers' output is sold and the second is that prices are market-determined and so will rise when there is a shortfall in supply.

Risk and incomplete markets, factors which, according to Smith and Thomson (1991) might justify intervention in the workings of the market, also complicate fertiliser supply. By raising a farmer's capital expenditure, purchasing fertiliser also increases his/her risk (especially in view of the fact that the full benefits of fertiliser will not be achieved unless there is adequate rainfall). Since farmers tend to be risk averse, fertiliser use will usually fall below the economically efficient level unless governments or other bodies intervene to bear some of the risk (cost) themselves (Smith and Thomson, 1994; Fontaine and Sindzingre, 1991).

Many farmers will not be able to purchase fertiliser unless they have access to credit before planting begins. Credit markets are, however, notoriously incomplete (see below). In the past this problem was often addressed through an 'integrated system' (Fontaine and Sindzingre, 1991) whereby marketing parastatals also supplied farmers with inputs or credit in kind. Their own risk was reduced by their monopoly position which put them in a privileged position for loan recovery and interest collection. They were able to deduct payments at source when purchasing farmers' crops. For this reason Fontaine and Sindzingre (1991) caution against over zealous 'network reforms' (reforms of the network of farmer supply mechanisms) and hesitantly suggest that some form of monopoly might be recommendable. They explicitly advise against applying theoretical microeconomic arguments about efficiency of markets to policy formulation.

It should be noted, however, that it is not just parastatal marketing monopolies which can provide credit and other services to their suppliers. Recent research conducted at Wye College of the University of London has shown the continuing importance of 'interlocked markets' in which private traders supply credit to those from whom they purchase goods (Poulton et al., 1997). This is obviously more complex when no formal monopoly exists; the traders must usually rely on their own knowledge of particular suppliers to assess their creditworthiness. Nevertheless, the importance of such informal financial service providers should not be under-estimated.

The possibility of groups or farmers' organisations working together to overcome some of the problems associated with credit markets is addressed below.

The final economic complication relates to the potential negative externalities of fertiliser use, in terms of pollution and contamination (both in use and during production). Although these problems may only become important after a certain volume threshold is surpassed in any area, they should certainly be taken into consideration when devising overall fertiliser policy. For example, government intervention may be necessary in order to extend 'best practices' for fertiliser use or to devise a regulatory framework for the manufacturing and supply of agrochemicals. Also important is research into organic fertilisation methods which reduce rather than increase the use of purchased inputs and are therefore unattractive to private companies. Neither private entrepreneurs nor farmers' organisations are likely to be the major suppliers of such advice. For private entrepreneurs it will rarely be profitable (except, possibly, for purchasing companies which gain a premium for organic produce) and farmers' organisations tend to concentrate in areas where they are able to provide clearly visible short-term benefits to their members (Carney, 1996).

2.3 Progress towards new goals

Given the imperfections in fertiliser markets, wholesale liberalisation might not, even theoretically, result in an overall improvement in efficiency. Direct payment by customers to private enterprises (here, those supplying fertiliser) should, though, increase accountability (as long as these enterprises have a relatively devolved decision-making structure and, preferably, some sort of performance-related pay system in place). The particular problem of timeliness of supply should be ameliorated as markets are liberalised so long as private traders actually control the timing of deliveries and are not dependent upon other unresponsive organisations (for example, government agencies which control imports) for their own supply.

Accounts of change in almost all the countries covered in the literature show that some elements of former interventionist government policies are retained under new systems. The extent to which full-scale liberalisation has been avoided because governments are aware of imperfections in the fertiliser market or wish to pursue objectives other than economic efficiency, rather than simply being unable to withdraw (either because private enterprise is not ready to step in or because of their own inertia), is not explicitly addressed in the literature.

Private traders have tended to concentrate on the retail side of fertiliser markets in countries such as Tanzania and Kenya (World Bank, 1994a). If market conditions worsen, exit from this side of the business tends to be easier. However, this also means that the private sector must continue to rely on public sector agencies as suppliers. This reduces their ability to enhance effectiveness as ultimate supplies are still in the hands of unresponsive institutions. Shepherd (1989) notes that public sector problems, such as late supply, have been replicated in cooperatives and amongst private traders. Furthermore the scope of gains in effectiveness and accountability are limited because the private sector itself is limited, especially by such factors as inadequate access to credit and foreign exchange and poor profit margins (Shepherd, 1989; Smith and Thomson, 1991; Bates, 1989).

2.4 Focus on the rural poor

Benefits to the rural poor deriving from change in the supply system for fertiliser are limited in the first instance by the fact that most subsistence farmers, especially those in Africa, continue not to use inorganic fertiliser. To the extent that they do use fertiliser or have an unmet demand for fertiliser it is unlikely that overall reforms in the system have benefited them. Since they are marginal users with a low ability to pay yet high service costs (due to spatial dispersion, poor transport systems to the remote areas in which they live and low overall demand) they tend to fall below the profit threshold for private suppliers of this bulky item (Smith and Thomson, 1991).

This last factor is common to the supply of all purchased inputs under discussion in this review. The problem is more intense the higher the transport costs involved in taking a particular good to a certain area (this in turn is a factor of both volume:value ratios and perishability) and the lower the willingness to pay for the good. In the past governments implicitly subsidised the poor who lived in remote areas – and hence increased their own popularity – by means of pan-territorial pricing policies. Such uniform pricing policies cannot, however, be retained once production (supply) is out of the hands of government as they will simply result in private traders failing to service rural areas where costs are high. On the other hand, if traders seek to maximise profits, such areas will probably be neglected anyway (as outlined above). The only way, then, for the government to *guarantee* supply to the poorer areas is to continue to provide the goods, or funding for the goods, itself on the grounds of equity (unless local groups or NGOs undertake this function).

Liberalisation of fertiliser markets has often taken place concurrently with cuts in subsidies. Farmers have suffered both because they have had to pay higher prices for their goods and because private traders have been deterred from entering a falling market. This observation is made by Richard Pearce (1992) about the situation in Ghana. It is only in exceptional circumstances that farmers may have benefited. These would arise if supply constraints prior to liberalisation had meant that effective purchase prices were way in excess of the official prices (for example in Nigeria parallel prices reached up to four times the official price (World Bank, 1994a)) or situations such as that noted by de Coninck and Tinguiri (1992) in Niger where official prices rose but were undercut by cheap imports from Nigeria. However, a new price which was double the former official price would still make fertiliser prohibitively expensive for most small farmers, regardless of how this new price related to the former parallel market price.

Aware of the negative correlation between price and demand, some governments, for example Tanzania, have nominally liberalised supply but retained some subsidies (World Bank, 1994a). The problem here is that the retention of subsidies essentially means the retention of public sector intervention in the supply system. Private traders are unlikely to be attracted by a market which is still severely distorted by government intervention (Shepherd, 1989). Even targeted subsidies are likely to result in 'leakage' into and hence distortion of the mainstream supply and a reduction in intended benefits to the poor (Fontaine and Sindzingre, 1991).

Another problem for smaller farmers is that they tend to be more risk averse and less eligible for credit than their larger counterparts. To the extent that the privatisation of fertiliser supply entails dismantling the 'integrated network' of input supply/marketing services/credit they therefore tend to lose out. In addition, their greater risk aversion implies a steeper decline in their demand if fertiliser prices rise.

2.5 Lessons

Liberalisation of fertiliser markets has not been easy to achieve. Governments, in both Africa and Asia, have been reluctant to step back from control of what they consider to be one of the key instruments for modernising agriculture and raising production. Since removal of subsidies has often – though not always – been shown to reduce demand their concerns may be well grounded (Shepherd, 1989; Kelly, 1988; Fontaine and Sindzingre, 1991). Furthermore, there are examples of continued fertiliser subsidies underpinning impressive advances in agricultural development (for example in Indonesia) which does nothing for the case of the reformers.

Private traders have been less willing to step in to fill the vacancies left by retreating governments than might have been expected, though part of this is due to the manner of public sector retreat. The debate about whether or to what extent entrepreneurs are waiting in the wings for the decision to 'unleash markets' (World Bank, 1994a) has been going on for some time (World Bank, 1989; Marsden, 1990; ODA, 1994) and is relevant not only to fertiliser supply but to almost all the areas under consideration in this paper.

Most authors concur in the fact that private trade might need a 'kick start' or some sort of infant industry protection. Piñeiro (1986) sees underdevelopment as 'characterized by a weak private sector' meaning that it is unrealistic to expect the private sector to take over former government activities without some positive encouragement. From Bangladesh Parish (1992) reports that while private traders existed at the time that the liberalisation programme got underway, there was a lack of viable mid-level businesses, between bazaar-type dealers and cartels which offered little improvement on government monopolies. Many states have spent decades trying to stamp out any vestiges of private trade which makes it unlikely that entrepreneurs will emerge the moment policy is reversed. This is particularly true in countries where traders have traditionally come from unpopular ethnic minorities and therefore have particular grounds for caution (Bates, 1989). At the very least, private traders will require evidence of consistent government policies and actions before they are willing to invest. Clearly some of the half-reforms and reversals detailed above do not provide this (Shepherd, 1989; Commander, 1989).

Another concern put forward by some authors is that instead of the efficiencies predicted by free-market economics, what emerges is a class of profiteering and exploitative businessmen who seek rather to find and safeguard monopolistic positions than to compete for normal profits (de Janvry and Sadoulet, 1993; Hewitt, 1992; Shepherd, 1989). If this proves to be the case in the long run, governments must be prepared to step in; close monitoring is therefore required.

Traders themselves require credit and inputs. Shepherd (1989) notes that credit tends not to be forthcoming for them for similar reasons that they might be unwilling to extend credit to farmers – lack of collateral. Thus, in Bangladesh, establishing a substantial commercial credit facility for the private sector was seen to be an essential step in the transition to private supply (Parish, 1992). This is, indeed, a growing area of focus for enterprise development programmes sponsored by donors. Traders depend upon a functioning transport and communication system. If they wish to import fertiliser they also require access to foreign exchange and import procedures which do not act as a major deterrent (Shepherd, 1989). Ultimately, though, unless they can be relatively sure of demand, they are unlikely to enter a business such as fertiliser supply which has high capital requirements and may require investment in infrastructure (such as storage facilities) to manage the very seasonal demand.

These conditions have seldom been met, particularly in the adjusting countries of sub-Saharan Africa. The economic environments in such countries tend to be very unstable. Successive devaluations severely affect the fortunes of importers. Demand for fertiliser is also linked to current crop prices; these may change rapidly during periods of transition. Hewitt (1992) reports that after adjustment began in Madagascar in 1982 fertiliser prices rose sixfold in six years. Although the paddy price also rose, the ratio of paddy price to NPK price still fell to 66% of pre-adjustment levels. One role for donors can therefore be to help domestic governments develop a coherent national fertiliser policy which helps stabilise the environment for private traders.

Certainly, if governments wish to pursue goals of enhanced equity or donors wish to support pro-poor development policies, more effective ways of ensuring the supply and use of fertiliser by the poor will have to be found. This will require further investigation on the feasibility and costs of targeting subsidies specifically to poorer groups of users. It will be important, at the same time, to help increase the stability of demand in poorer areas and improve the efficiency of fertiliser use (which should further increase demand). Sometimes this can be done indirectly through improving farmers' access to new varieties of crops or to marketing facilities and services which help stabilise output prices and thus make fertiliser use more attractive (for example, local grain depots).

It can also be done by improving fertiliser use recommendations and making them more relevant to poor farmers' conditions. Fertiliser recommendations in many countries tend to be formulated for large areas without taking into account the interactions between organic and inorganic fertilisers, the response rates of various crops (including intercrops) and the importance of different micro-nutrients (attention is usually focused only on N, P and K). Such recommendations are usually based on station trails rather than on-farm work which takes into account farmers' particular circumstances and socio-economic or physical constraints. One important way of raising demand for fertiliser will therefore be to refine the recommendations to raise the overall productivity of fertiliser use.

3. Seed supply

3.1 Changes in supply or supplier

Seed supply can usefully be divided into three different aspects. The first is research into new or improved types of seeds, conducted both domestically and internationally. The second is the physical supply of seeds themselves, either wholesale or retail, and the third is regulation (including rules governing variety testing, variety regulation and seed quality control, see Tripp et al., 1997). There is no reason why the same institution should be responsible for all functions, though governments, in conjunction with national and international public sector research institutions frequently have been so. Even after liberalisation most governments retain responsibility for basic, as opposed to adaptive research though they may cede control over 'near-market' research (Brenner, 1991)[1].

Non-governmental bodies (NGOs, private institutions etc.) may also perform all three of the tasks mentioned above, though some aspects of regulation are likely to remain at least funded by government. It is rare for private sector organisations to restrict themselves to research alone – unless they do so under contract to another organisation – as the money to fund research is usually generated from product sales (the second aspect of supply). While NGOs may be less concerned about sales than commercial companies, it remains the case that they must ensure dissemination of their research findings if they are to be effective in their efforts. They usually, therefore, sponsor seed multiplication programmes to capitalise upon any research they undertake (Cromwell et al., 1993).

Otherwise organisations can operate only at the level of physical supply – producing seeds using technology which has been developed by (usually) public institutions. At the limit this might imply the type of exclusive on-growing contract that the Zimbabwe government used to hold with the Seed Co-op (Cromwell, 1992). At the other end of the spectrum are small and medium-sized companies and individual farmers which specialise in growing seed for local markets – relying not on exclusivity, but on reliability of supply and high quality, to secure sales (Brenner, 1991).

Bangladesh provides an example of a traditional public sector seed supply system which was designed to provide an integrated service but ended up providing little service at all. The Bangladesh Agricultural Development Corporation (BADC) was overgrown, provided poor quality goods and services and, as a monopoly, was unresponsive to farmers' needs. Farmers were therefore forced to rely on locally produced seed and illegal imports from India (Huntings, 1994). Recognition of the

---

[1] It should be noted that very little basic agricultural research – meaning research that is unfocused and pioneering – is conducted in developing countries, and that much of the debate in this area is therefore somewhat academic.

shortcomings of such large and unresponsive parastatal seed enterprises has resulted in major changes in the seed supply networks in many countries.

In Bangladesh a new Seed Policy was devised in 1990. This explicitly called for private sector involvement (in both research and supply) and encouraged BADC to act as a wholesaler rather than a retailer. A new Seed Wing was created in the Ministry of Agriculture to monitor the progress of the reforms and to provide services to the whole system, but particularly the private sector. The Department of Agricultural Extension was charged with the responsibility of feeding back information on farmers' needs. Overall support was to be provided by various donors (Huntings, 1994).

This last factor – donor support and/or pressure for reform – is common to the seed sectors of many countries. For example, in the Gambia seed reform was part of the 1985 Economic Recovery Programme. The public sector monopoly on groundnut seed was lifted and the private sector was expected to take over seed supply in the long term (though Cromwell et al. (1993) argued that at least by the early 1990s it had not yet taken on a major role). In the interim donors were to support NGO and government seed projects. An FAO fertiliser project, for example, was designed to encourage groups of farmers to multiply seeds, to spur private sector development.

Where donors are not involved, international influences often come in the form of multinational seed companies such as Cargill and Pioneer. The literature covered here does not suggest that these companies *force* the opening up of seed sectors in various countries. However, authors such as Grobman (1992) argue that in countries where the seed markets are large enough to be attractive to multinationals, these will soon dominate unless governments specifically promote domestic companies. Multinationals have a particular advantage in research because they can spread its high costs over the many markets in which they operate and transfer technology from one to another. Domestic companies, which tend to be more resource constrained, usually limit themselves to seed multiplication and supply, where their local knowledge can give them a competitive advantage. Often the two types of company form partnerships to capitalise on joint strengths. Indeed, in certain countries multinationals are obliged to link up with domestic companies if they wish to enter the market.

In Turkey, considered one of the success stories of seed market liberalisation, more than thirty foreign companies now operate in conjunction with local partners. Before liberalisation in Turkey only 1.5% of total seed production was in private hands. Five years later, in 1990, 96% of hybrid maize was produced by private companies (Dalrymple and Srivastava, 1994; Srivastava and Jaffee, 1993). Governments, for their part, might recognise the advantage of association with multinationals. Thus, in 1988 the Malawi government sold a controlling interest in ADMARC, the state-owned seed distribution company to Cargill (Cromwell, 1992).

The role of NGOs, both international and domestic, in the seed sector varies enormously. Cromwell et al. (1993) studied the activities of eighteen NGOs in nine countries. These activities ranged from multiplication of non-accredited seeds with no local testing to the establishment of formal, local breeding programmes. In almost all cases seed was sold to final users, though frequently at prices below those prevailing in the market (which would, amongst other things, deter private commercial suppliers from entering the market).

Farmers' organisations are also active in the seed sector, particularly in areas where government supply has failed. As noted above, successful supply of physical inputs to members can be an effective way of enhancing member loyalty, hence group cohesion and the scope for collective action. While smaller organisations are likely to operate only at the level of semi-formal supply, the larger and richer farmers' associations can conduct their own research. For example, Seed Co-op in Zimbabwe runs its own research station (despite also having exclusive rights to seeds developed by the NARS) and invests 1.5–1.75% of its turnover in research. In Ecuador, the NGO CESA (the Ecuadorian Centre for Agricultural Services) helps farmer associations with seed production (Bebbington and Farrington, 1992 Bebbington et al., 1993). Formerly CESA had to compete with private operators for access to seed produced from INIAP (the Ecuadorian national agricultural research institute), but in 1991 it signed an agreement for preferential access (Cromwell et al., 1993).

The third important aspect of seed supply is regulation. There are at least three distinct activities which are often confounded under this single heading. These are: (i) the management of variety testing in public sector plant breeding; (ii) variety regulation (registration, performance testing and release); and (iii) seed quality control. Within the latter category there are again two distinct activities: seed certification and seed testing. The former is the verification of genetic quality which provides an assurance that the seed is of the specified variety and is of sufficient genetic purity. The latter relates to assessing physical characteristics such as analytical purity and germination capacity (Tripp et al., 1997). Other dimensions of seed quality control include attention to storage and marketing conditions and assessment of standards at the point of delivery. This is required for all seeds as a protection for customers, given the dangers of adverse selection and moral hazard (see next section). Nevertheless, quality standards should not be unduly high or onerous as this can impose unnecessary costs on seed producers and, ultimately, consumers.

Seed certification must be sponsored by the public sector, though it can be actually performed by a private organisation, as it is in the USA (Grobman, 1992). The Zambia Seed Company – a commercial organisation which nonetheless remains in the public sector – is monitored through the Seed Control and Certification Institute. This is currently a public body, but Cromwell (1992) argues that were it allowed to retain the fees which it collects it could become financially autonomous.

Seed testing can be performed by the public sector – indeed Grobman (1992) argues that the government must have a role in this and should perform spot checks on producers' output. Tripp et al. (1997), however, point out the importance of involving the commercial seed sector in defining the management practices or standards which are used. Visible quality control mechanisms are often used by companies to try to distinguish themselves from their competitors in order to gain commercial advantage. In Turkey companies responsible for about 10% of seed production are members of the Seed Industry Association which regulates itself in conjunction with the Ministry of Agriculture. Unfortunately regulation for non-members remains rather haphazard which increases the risk to purchasers (Dalrymple and Srivastava, 1994). In Peru Srivastava and Jaffee (1993) report the existence of almost thirty private companies which have entered the market since liberalisation began in 1980. These account for a rapidly increasing proportion of overall seed supply. Quality control is provided by regional seed associations (which also provide technical support to farmers who wish to grow seed themselves), four out of eight of which are self-sustaining.

Cromwell et al. (1993) report that about half the NGOs they studied execute strict quality control testing while one quarter are nominally linked to government quality-control agencies. These may or may not have the resources to reach the scattered NGO production sites, especially since the demand for quality control services tends to be highly seasonal. A particular problem may occur if the public sector refuses to cede its responsibility for quality control yet does not have the financial resources to cover the costs of its visits. In such a case as this the elevated cost of the central quality-control agency may be transferred to the NGOs or small enterprises concerned, with severe negative impacts.

Table 3 (taken from Tripp et al., 1997) summarises the options for monitoring seed quality control. The authors stress the importance not only of establishing the right systems for quality control but also of ensuring that the regulations can be enforced. From the customer's point of view, a key issue is the extent to which those who contravene the regulations can be 'punished' either through the courts or through the market (by withdrawing custom). This reinforces the issue raised earlier of the accountability that is built in to the market mechanism; in a competitive market those who do not adhere to quality standards are easily punished. Though there may be some delay since, with seeds, poor quality may not be evident until germination or even the end of the growing cycle.

Table 3: Options for monitoring seed quality control

Option	Justifications	Concerns
• Conventional certification by a public sector regulatory agency	• Government control for main food crops • Necessary when seed production monopoly exists (e.g. parastatal) • Provides technical assistance, particularly if seed growers are dispersed and/or inexperienced • Often required for seed export	• Allows little flexibility in standards • High costs • Limited coverage and participation • Possibilities for corruption
• Certification by an independent certification agency	• Allows seed producers and consumers the option of certification • Permit flexibility in standards	• Depends on consumer understanding of certification • Requires sufficient demand to pay for private certification service
• Quality control tasks shared between regulatory agency, seed producers and merchants (through Quality Declared Seed*, delegating authority, or licensing)	• Encourages development of quality control capacity • Less expensive • Allows wide coverage • Permits flexibility in standards	• Requires good capacity for spot checks • Requires clear enforcement strategies • Requires technical capacity for seed producers and merchants
• Truthful labelling[‡]: seed producers and merchants monitor seed quality with regulatory agency oversight	• Seed producer responsible for seed quality • Allows standards to respond to market demand • Encourages diversification • Costs borne by seed producers	• Needs strong, independent enforcement capacity • Assumes well-functioning market and competition • Should not be confused with lower standards • Still requires supervisory oversight

* The concept of Quality Declared Seed (QDS) was developed by the FAO to provide guidelines for establishing a seed regulatory system that could be operated with limited resources (FAO, 1993). Under this system, the regulatory agency randomly samples a small percentage of seed production plots each year, rather than attempting to inspect all of them. Sampling from a percentage of sales points is suggested as well. Such a system can begin to shift responsibility for quality control to seed producers and merchants. The system does, however, require a well-defined enforcement strategy.

‡ A very straightforward option for seed quality control is truthful labelling. The minimum standards (for purity, germination, etc.) for truthfully labelled seed may be determined by the state regulatory agency, or may be left to the discretion of the seed producer. Consumers bear an important responsibility for monitoring adherence to standards and reporting complaints, while

regulatory agencies may play an oversight role and carry out spot checks. The enforcement of truthful labelling may be the responsibility of the courts or the regulatory agency. The principal distinguishing feature of this system is that the regulatory agency plays little role in the direct supervision of seed production. It is up to the seed producer to ensure that the seed meets the minimum standards described on the label.

3.2 Economic analysis

Seed technology is subtractable, but except in the special case of hybrids, it is not excludable. Open-pollinated varieties can be reproduced by farmers themselves and passed on through the very active informal seed distribution mechanisms which exist in most areas. This makes them common pool goods (Umali and Schwartz, 1994).

There are clearly no barriers to private companies researching into or producing such seeds. Brenner (1991) identifies private companies in three out of four of the countries which she studied (Thailand, Brazil and Mexico) which do just this and Venkatesan and Schwartz (1992) argue that private companies tend to favour seeds research as an entry point into the whole area of agricultural research. However, private companies will often not find it economically attractive to produce seeds of open-pollinated varieties, unless they have clear advantages in terms of quality and reliability of supply which enable them consistently to capture significant market share.

Brenner (1991) suggests that larger companies are generally interested in producing open-pollinated varieties only while they are in the process of developing hybrids. Rather than looking for a sustainable profit stream from their early products, they use open-pollinated varieties to establish a reputation and develop their distribution mechanisms. Otherwise it is mostly just small, localised firms with low overheads which are willing to compete in the market for open-pollinated varieties against the vigorous competition posed by farmers' own supply. However, this is not always the case, as Beynon and Mbogoh (1996) discovered in Kenya. There, Kenya Breweries has been conducting its own research into malting barley since 1978. Changes in Kenyan seed legislation in 1994 mean that Kenya Breweries can now grow and distribute seed (previously these tasks were monopolised by the Kenya Seed Company) and that there is a certain degree of varietal protection in place. Although malting barley is open pollinated, the company has calculated that farmers will need to replace their seed every 3–4 years if they are to maintain their yields. This rate of replacement should be adequate to cover Kenya Breweries' research costs.

In the absence of companies such as Kenya Breweries which are willing to become involved in the supply of open-pollinated varieties, some intervention in the seed sector is likely to be required, whether by government or non-profit organisations. Farmer retention and informal seed distribution will always account for a majority of the seed sown each year in developing countries (Cromwell et al., 1993). However, there should still be at least one alternative source of seed available to farmers, not least because in the worst years or when there is civil strife farmers are often forced against their will to eat their stored seed (Sperling et al.,1996).

Governments themselves can become suppliers. They can also, arguably, intervene to make open-pollinated varieties more attractive to private companies. This brings up the whole issue of intellectual property rights and patent protection (Grobman, 1992; Evenson and David, 1993). Some developed countries have systems of plant-breeders rights in operation, but Brenner (1991) questions whether these could be enforceable in developing countries and Dalrymple and Srivastava (1994) suggest that they might not be appropriate until the seed industry has reached a certain level of maturity. Before this time, they argue, added regulation would be more likely to stifle than encourage creativity.

Hybrids, on the other hand, demonstrate qualities of what Brenner (1991) refers to as 'patent-like protection'. Their full benefits can only be captured by farmers if new seed is purchased each season and they can therefore be considered to be private goods. Thus the reach of hybrids in any country will, other things being equal, determine the involvement of the private sector. Where hybrids are suitable for cultivation, farmers are only likely to be willing to pay the relatively high prices required to recoup companies' development costs, if quality control is stringent. Hybrid-producing companies thus have an incentive to regulate their own quality and little intervention by government should be required (except, perhaps, to prevent counterfeiting by others).

However, for other companies and in production of lower cost seeds, the adverse selection and moral hazard problems are expected to be significant. Adverse selection is the economic name given to the problem which occurs when purchasers, unlike vendors, are not able to judge the value of the good at the time at which the sale is made (Umali et al., 1992). Except where seed is obviously damaged, farmers will be unable to judge how it will perform when planted and therefore their purchase will be more risky than is desirable. This might lead them to under-invest (Smith and Thomson, 1991). Complicating matters further is the fact that even if the seed appears to fail, other factors (weather, soil conditions, pests etc.) might be blamed – this introduces moral hazard. Because the performance of the seed depends not only on its own quality but also upon a range of other factors which are out of the control of the vendor, it is not possible for the vendor to attach a guarantee to the seed at the point of sale. While such problems are not entirely soluble, government regulation can help (Grobman, 1992). In general, Smith and Thomson (1991) note that governments have a competitive advantage in regulation because of their legitimacy in coercion, although transaction costs associated with regulation can in some cases, they argue, outweigh its benefits.

Other concerns which might militate towards continued government intervention in the seeds sector relate to the protection of genetic diversity through seed breeding programmes or support to in situ conservation and the nature of basic, as opposed to applied, research (addressed in the following section).

3.3 Progress towards new goals

The entry of new suppliers into the seed sector has, in general, benefited farmers by improving the variety as well as the sheer quantity of seeds available (Srivastava and Jaffee, 1993). For example in Mexico poorer farmers who receive subsidies for seed purchases can now chose between public and private sector varieties (Brenner, 1991). Private companies are also reported to be more responsive to farmers' needs and to give more technical advice with their seed sales (Srivastava and Jaffee, 1993).

Public sector organisations are not, however, necessarily non-functional. Cromwell (1992) characterises the public sector (though commercially oriented) Zambia Seed Company as 'an efficient and reasonably effective seed organisation'. Perhaps the greatest difficulty with public sector seed organisations is that they have always attempted often with little success to provide national coverage. This Cromwell (1992) notes is likely to be far more expensive and difficult than running a series of regional seed networks.

One fact noted by a number of authors (Brenner, 1991; Dalrymple and Srivastava, 1994) is that individual researchers will be more productive in the private sector because of their greater access to resources. Brenner (1991) illustrates this by analysing Mexican maize research budgets in 1987. Twenty five private seed companies together spent $1.7m on research, equivalent to $113,000 for each research station and $61,000 for each scientist. The National Research Institute's maize budget was less than half this amount, despite the fact that it was supporting the same number of research stations and three times as many scientists (though there is no suggestion that simply raising the amount of resources available to public sector researchers would solve all their productivity problems).

A study by Echeverria cited in Dalrymple and Srivastava (1994) shows that tropical countries in which multinational corporations are conducting more research have a higher yield of maize. The suggestion is that the involvement of the private sector improves the efficiency of the seed sector, although the extent to which the effect is due to hybrid density rather than private sector involvement, *per se*, is not very clear. In any case, overall efficiency gains may be reduced if the public sector refuses to withdraw from areas where the private sector is active. Brenner (1991) argues that the public sector may want to 'keep up' with private work on hybrids, for example, as this may represent the cutting edge of research.[2] The result is wasteful duplication. Public sector organisations in some countries, such as Mexico, have, though, demonstrated a willingness to withdraw. The Mexican seed parastatal was established in 1960 with a mandate over twenty three crops. In 1989 this was cut to just the four main staples: maize, rice, beans and wheat.

---

[2] This is a particular problem in the area of biotechnology research. Public sector research organisations are often very unwilling to abnegate all responsibility for such research, yet they rarely have the resources to make important contributions in this very costly area of work.

Where NGOs have recognised that farmers' needs are not being met they have sometimes stepped into this role in an attempt to improve the effectiveness of overall seed supply. Despite some notable successes (e.g. Mitti et al., 1997) Cromwell et al. (1993) criticise NGOs for basing their intervention more on their own policy agendas than on a sophisticated understanding of the needs of the communities with which they are working. It is vital to understand the nature of seed demand and why farmers are seeking seed off farm before designing any response. If farmers are simply seeking new varieties this may require just an initial introduction of new seed. If they have seed quality or management problems it may be more appropriate to provide extension advice to improve farm-level seed management than to provide support to external seed supply enterprises. If purchase is an indication of poverty-induced seed shortage this is unlikely to be addressed by conventional seed provision activities. Unless these differences are understood and responses are designed appropriately the full potential efficiency gains of changes in supply are unlikely to be forthcoming.

NGO attempts at seed supply have been further complicated by mixed relief/development motives (Cromwell et al., 1993). In general, the 'third sector' has been criticised for failure to coordinate with other agencies and a rather unsystematic approach which has prevented it from understanding who is gaining and who is losing from the seed supply mechanisms which it supports. Together these problems may reduce the scope for sustainability in NGO projects after external funding and expertise are withdrawn. However, the extent of this problem should not be overestimated. Some NGOs have established very effective systems for the supply of planting material. For example, in north east Uganda the NGO Vision Terudo (amongst others) has established an impressive programme to supply farmers whose livelihoods were devastated by the war and unrest in that area with new strains of cassava resistant to African Cassava Mosaic Virus. In the first year a farmer is allocated a certain amount of planting material. He/she then bulks this up and returns the same amount to the NGO for distribution elsewhere. Surplus planting material and the tubers can be sold or used locally (usually to the benefit of a community group). From the second year onwards the farmer can continue with his/her own commercial supply enterprise.

As a result of examples such as this and the dismal state of public sector seed enterprises pre-reform, the clear consensus in the literature is that the seed sector, and farmers in general, will benefit from the involvement of various different types of actor. It has already been noted that only when there is competition between different seed suppliers will farmers be able to 'punish' those selling poor quality seeds through the market (by withdrawing their custom). However, competition should not be courted without some consideration of capacity. It is not a simple matter to ensure the supply of quality planting material on a consistent basis to a wide range of clients in a situation of uncertain demand (these characteristics are common to many rural areas). The difficulties are particularly severe for crops such as sweet potato (where there may be a long gap between harvesting and replanting) and sorghum (sorghum seed is particularly susceptible to storage problems). Efforts to support the very poorest households – which have few resources and skills upon which to draw – to develop micro-seed enterprises are therefore unlikely to succeed.

3.4 Focus on the rural poor

In much the same way that most of the poorest farmers do not use fertilisers, many of them are also outside the formal seed supply system. If they rarely buy seeds (only about 20% of seeds used in developing countries are produced by formal suppliers (Cromwell et al., 1993)), changes in the formal seed system will have very little impact upon them. However, this is not always the case. It has been shown in some places that it is exactly the poorest who do purchase seed as it is these people who are most likely to be forced to eat their saved seed during the 'hungry period' (Sperling et al., 1996). If, therefore, new suppliers are able to supply seed at lower cost and in more appropriate package sizes, then these poor people will certainly benefit from change.

In particular they are likely to benefit from reforms in seed regulation which reduce the costs of producing seed. If seed certification by a designated, central agency is mandatory, costs incurred can be high as a limited number of agency staff will have to make multiple visits to dispersed production plots. If, on the other hand, a range of different agencies become involved in quality control through agreed licensing systems and truthful labelling schemes (with the public sector retaining the right to make spot checks), the costs incurred by seed producers can be significantly reduced (Tripp et al., 1997)

Direct efforts to expand the basis of seed production will, as noted above, rarely benefit the poorest. This is because of lack of capacity within the poorest households to multiply seed on a significant scale and to an acceptable quality. Even NGO projects have tended to support richer farmers who have this capacity to multiply seeds for local supply. Otherwise they have built on traditional supply mechanisms which have often been dominated by local elites (Cromwell et al., 1993). This is, nonetheless a realistic strategy. Poor people may gain indirectly if local suppliers provide seed suited to their immediate environment at a reasonable cost.

In countries where the private commercial sector is active there has nevertheless been a tendency for it to focus either on hybrid seeds or on richer areas. Indeed Brenner (1991) notes that in both Mexico and Brazil both private and public systems focused on more favoured areas. In parallel with the fertiliser sector, traders are unwilling or unable to meet the needs of smaller farmers by providing tiny quantities of seed in remote areas. Cromwell (1992) argues that private companies are unable to extend their reach by cross-subsidising sales to more remote areas with resources generated from sales to richer areas because of the power of the richer farmers themselves. This suggests that it will be very small scale local suppliers who will succeed in the remoter areas.

There is little evidence in the literature of government using the period of liberalisation to refocus its own efforts on poorer farmers (having withdrawn from those areas which are attractive to the private sector). Neither does the issue of the relative costs of privately and publicly produced seeds receive much attention. It is therefore impossible to draw general conclusions as to whether seeds have become more accessible and more affordable – the two criteria which Srivastava and Jaffee (1993) single out as being of critical importance – as a result of liberalisation. Certainly in Zimbabwe small farmers do not benefit from the fact that the government has granted long-term rights for reproduction of government-researched seed to the Seed Co-op which is controlled by large scale commercial farmers. As a virtual monopoly Seed Co-op operates a cost-plus pricing arrangement but appointed distributors have developed cartels based upon geographic monopolies and have raised prices still higher. Past government attempts at price control have simply resulted in a decline in supply in rural areas (Cromwell, 1992).

Overall, it seems clear that if poorer farmers are really to benefit they will require training schemes, run by either government or NGOs, which help them improve the quality of the seed they grow themselves (though they will use this for home consumption only) (Cromwell et al., 1993). Providing support to local seed enterprise development will also remain an important strategy for reaching the poor.

3.5 Lessons

Many of the lessons to be learned from early efforts at reform in the seed sector are similar to those in the fertiliser sector. The most obvious of these is that reform will tend disproportionately to benefit the relatively better off farmers unless special safeguards for the poor are built in. A second is that the government might need to provide some active encouragement to private traders if reforms are to increase the availability of seed (Cromwell, 1992).

Strong seasonality in seed supply means that traders have to carry large inventories of often highly perishable goods for which they need adequate storage facilities. Entry therefore requires a significant amount of capital, which Grobman (1992) argues the government might need to provide, at concessional interest rates. Governments can also not expect private traders to enter markets which are still subject to severe distortions. For example in Malawi liberalisation began as part of the first structural adjustment loan of 1981. By the late 1980s few private traders had established businesses since prices were still controlled and margins were therefore insufficiently attractive, especially given the very poor transport infrastructure in the country (Cromwell, 1992). Dalrymple and Srivastava (1994) report that in both India and Pakistan the development of the private sector has been severely impeded by subsidies to the public sector and very low official prices, although they also note that both countries provide tax incentives to companies which conduct research.

Another lesson common to the two sectors is that the complexity of existing systems and linkages between sectors should not be underestimated when planning reform, as this might lead to unexpected results. Thus, when the seed market in Zambia was liberalised in 1990 and the Provincial Co-operative Unions there lost their position as monopsonistic purchasers they also lost their access to credit. Instead of facing up to new and potentially beneficial competitive influences (they tended to be very corrupt) they ended up unable to purchase seed at all. Some seed was sold through other bodies, such as NGOs, but these were new to the business and not well organised and general seed availability fell (Cromwell, 1992). Private traders failed to step forward partly because the margins to be made in agricultural trade were perceived to be very low.

Problems of sequencing of reform have also been evident in the seed sector (Cromwell, 1992). Seed purchases, like fertiliser purchases, will be affected by the price paid to farmers for their crops. Where these do not rise as fast as seed prices, demand for purchased seed will fall. During a period of rapid change in Malawi the producer and seed prices for groundnuts converged and seed ended up being consumed as food. In Zimbabwe, on the other hand, producer prices for all varieties of sunflower seed were the same which meant that farmers had no incentive to purchase the seeds of varieties with a higher oil content. Such a situation damaged both the seed suppliers and the government as the purchaser of inferior grade sunflower seeds. Availability of fertiliser will also have a significant effect upon demand for modern seed varieties (Cromwell, 1992).

Finally, all authors emphasise that the public sector role in the seed sector will always remain, especially in small and poor countries which would not be attractive to multinationals even were markets to be liberalised (Dalrymple and Srivastava, 1994). Market imperfections, especially those relating to non-hybrid seeds, are sufficiently great that wholesale privatisation of the seed industry would be likely to result in huge gaps in supply and regulation. The scattered efforts of NGOs and farmers organisations would not adequately fill these (Farrington and Bebbington, 1993) nor compensate for the loss of the reach of the old-style parastatals (Cromwell, 1992).

It may therefore remain appropriate for donors to support public plant breeding. However, it will be important to take into consideration the changed environment in which the public sector operates. In particular, it should be ensured that there is a clearly specified division of labour, and meaningful collaboration where relevant, between the public and the private sectors and that the public system is efficiently organised to identify and release varieties suited to a wide range of growing conditions.

Under certain circumstances emergency seed provision may also be required. It should, however, be ensured that such provision is motivated by genuine need rather than political considerations and that it takes adequate account of, and does not undermine, local seed supply systems or the efforts of newly established entrepreneurs.

4. Agricultural research systems

4.1 Changes in supply or supplier

The outputs of national agricultural research institutes, the traditional suppliers of formal research in developing countries, are increasingly being supplemented by private, cooperative or NGO research efforts (as well as by the efforts of farmers who have always been involved in their own research but whose contribution has only recently been recognised). Following Hobbs and Taylor's analysis of private research in Kenya, six different types of supplier of agricultural research can be identified (Hobbs and Taylor, 1987). Some, but not all, are also involved in extension.

The first type are multinationals which conduct commodity-specific research for major – often export – crops. They tend to be most active in plant breeding research although some also work on agronomic issues and conduct extension. As an example Hobbs and Taylor cite BAT which, at the time of writing, employed nine tobacco researchers and one hundred and fifty extensionists in Kenya.

The second type are national companies. Hobbs and Taylor suggest that these might be driven into research at times when lack of foreign exchange limits imports. Thus Kenya Breweries, faced with a crisis over imports of malting barley, developed its own local variety.

The third type are family enterprises. Because of limited resources, these do not engage in any extensive research but they might at times employ certain individuals to help them solve specific problems. The advantage that they have over their competitors is their closeness to and knowledge of product markets. This enables them to pinpoint very specifically what they are aiming to achieve, making their research very focused and usually fairly short-term.

The fourth type are commodity boards. These can be important sources of research and extension for the key export commodities in a country or region. For example, the Tea Research Foundation of Southern African countries, based in Malawi, is considered to be at the forefront of tea research (Venkatesan and Schwartz, 1992). Research is usually paid for by a cess on commodity sales which gives these autonomous institutes a reliable source of funds enabling them to conduct longer term research than some of their private counterparts (particularly the smaller organisations which operate in a single country/market).

The fifth type are non-governmental or non-profit organisations. These usually conduct research as part of integrated research/extension and rural support programmes. For example in Bangladesh the Mennonite Central Committee conducts research on soya production and then operates training programmes in marketing and extension. Bebbington and Farrington (1992) found that most NGO research is concentrated at the adaptive end of the research spectrum – NGOs take new technologies (often from the public sector) and adapt them to suit local needs. However, there are also examples of NGO research, such as that conducted by the Bharatiya Agro-Industries Foundation (BAIF) on artificial insemination in India, which is both long-term and ground-breaking.

In the final category are farmers themselves. It is clear that farmers conduct their own research, to varying degrees. The challenge for other researchers is to identify and build on this, where possible, rather than to sweep it aside or ignore it (Okali et al., 1994). The exact nature of farmers' experimentation has recently come under serious scrutiny by Sumberg and Okali (1997). These authors argue that farmer experimentation is rife, but that it is generally highly situation-specific and adaptive. They are therefore in some doubt about the 'synergy' between this type of experimentation and that derived from formal science (though they do agree that the many small changes wrought through farmer experimentation can, over time, alter entire farming systems).

While all these types of supplier can work on their own, partnerships which combine the different skills of the various suppliers may well be more fruitful and sustainable. In Zambia commercial farmers and commodity organisations together own and manage a 700 hectare research farm (Venkatesan and Schwartz, 1992) while in Mali Ceiba-Geigy has supported the establishment of an agricultural research station in conjunction with the public sector research system. In general, NGO/public sector partnerships, especially in on-farm research are becoming more common (Bebbington and Farrington, 1992). Indeed an increasing amount of donor money has been put into supporting such public-private partnerships, especially through the establishment of agricultural research funds which favour collaborative work (Carney, 1997).

Such funds which often cede significant decision-making power to user representatives are expected to increase both efficiency and accountability. They should open up a new centre of influence for users (who can be given a formal role in fund allocation) and a forum for dialogue about research priorities (USAID, 1996). In this way a number of the problems that have constrained further involvement of users and their organisations in technology generation and transfer can be 'solved'. In particular poorer farmers have been held back by their lack of financial leverage and their organisations have been hampered by poor financial structures and systems (Carney, 1996). Bringing farmer representatives into the management of dedicated technology funds provides them with a direct influence over technology budgets. It has the benefit of doing this without putting undue (and perhaps fatal) strains on the financial management systems of farmers' organisations (though the existence of efficient financial management systems within the organisation administering the fund is a precondition for fund effectiveness, this organisation is only rarely likely to be a farmers' organisation). The competition that is encouraged within many types of funds is intended to reward those whose research is generally productive and relevant to clients' needs and to overcome the problems posed by traditional allocation mechanisms for research and financing which are based on patronage, seniority or other criteria with little relevance to performance.

By providing a measure of stability, the opportunity for multiple donors to work together, and a source of funding which is not subject to the vagaries of domestic budget processes, dedicated technology funds are also expected to extend the planning horizon for research organisations. In principle, the most attractive model for technology funds would be one in which donors and others provided large endowments which would then yield an annual, sustainable income to fund research. However, most bilateral donors are not currently able or willing to establish such foundations and the majority of existing funds are 'reducing' (not internally sustainable) with the exception of those that are funded through producer levies.

In Latin America another hybrid source of agricultural research and extension has emerged in the form of externally-funded agricultural development foundations. Since 1984 at least five such foundations have been established with the assistance of USAID. These are specifically science-based institutions which support both public and private research and extension programmes in addition to conducting their own work. For example FUNDAGRO in Ecuador works with the national research service and FENECAFE (the Federation of coffee cooperatives) to improve the cultivation of coffee. It provides coordinators for the extension programme and funding for operational expenditures (Coutu and O'Donnell, 1991; Umali and Schwartz, 1994).

One other change in supply, rather than supplier, results from the efforts that some governments have been making to decentralise their own national research systems in order to make them more responsive to local needs. For example Mali's Commission on Decentralisation mandated the creation of regional centres with financial and administrative autonomy within the IER (Institut d'Economie Rurale), the main institute for agricultural research (Collion, 1994). In Israel regional R&D authorities are operated as independent units. They draw on sources of local funding although the Ministry of Agriculture, which provides the remainder of the funding does also draw up a list of national research priorities (Blum, 1991). In Chile, the Agricultural Research Institute (INIA) contracts research through regional Centres for Adaptation and Transfer of Technology drawing in both farmers' organisations and NGOs (Ashby and Sperling, 1994). Similarly, in Tanzania the Department of Research and Training has recently ceded financial authority to zonal level and is on the point of establishing Zonal Agricultural Research Funds (with donor support, anticipated to commence in early 1998).

4.2 Economic analysis

Like seeds, different types of agricultural research exhibit different economic characteristics. Once again the pivotal issues are appropriability and saleability of the results of research. Hobbs and Taylor (1987) distinguish between mechanical, chemical, biological and agronomic research. These they consider to be in a descending order of attractiveness to the private sector, according to their economic characteristics. At one extreme, mechanical technology is highly excludable and subtractable. At the other lies basic agronomic research which has neither of these attributes. Private sector companies will, therefore, be reluctant to invest in it; with no intervention this will result in a socially sub-optimal supply of the goods (Smith and Thomson, 1991; Umali and Schwartz, 1994). In most developing countries, however, a lack of human and financial resources means that basic research is not conducted domestically, rather it is 'imported' in product form or through the international system especially the International Agricultural Research Centres of the Consultative Group on International Agricultural Research (CGIAR).

Evenson (cited in Pray and Echeverria, 1991) distinguishes types of technology not by their subject, but by their stage. He talks of pre-technology, prototype technology and usable technology. The private sector focuses on the last of these. The government, Evenson believes, should play a role at each stage. This is because private firms base their investment decisions not only upon the degree of appropriable gains from research but also on market factors and technological opportunities for innovation (Pray and Echeverria, 1991). Government intervention is thus justified not simply to remedy public goods problems, but also to stimulate the flow of technology in the market and to help overcome the most difficult technological barriers which might otherwise reduce private sector research.

According to Evenson, pre-technology is a public good and therefore requires full government support. Prototype technology may be a private good but if markets or firms are small (which is often the case in developing countries) then some government support is likely to be required – particularly to mitigate the risk of large investments in research. Usable technology (so long as it is also saleable) is a private good; government involvement here is limited to the promotion of technological competition through enhancing the functioning of the market (Pray and Echeverria, 1991).

Once again, no authors put forward the view that the government should withdraw from research-related activities entirely. Rather, they stress the potential complementarities of different sources of research. Cleaver (1993) suggests that these will only be fully realised if a national agricultural research masterplan is drawn up. Such a plan would serve to consolidate and define all the various research efforts conducted by government, universities, donors and the six different types of private supplier identified above and in so doing would lay out the scope for collaboration. It would also provide information to help the refocusing of government research efforts, on the understanding that the government acts almost as a supplier of last resort. (Unfortunately, though, in places where such plans have been drawn up – such as Tanzania – there has often been a problem of lack of ownership by the key stakeholders and also lack of operational relevance because of the misalignment between regional research priorities and the national research masterplan.)

Such a reorientation and functional reorganisation of public sector research is also called for by Piñeiro (1986). As private companies begin to dominate the market for 'usable technology' (which functions reasonably efficiently), the public sector must focus upstream on public goods provision. He warns that unless this is done at a national level, private domestic companies will suffer in relation to multinationals. He discusses whether the public sector should become a direct supplier to private research, responding to particular requests, and concludes that, given the weakness of many public institutions, this should be the case. Since public institutions are so far removed from the needs of the customer, they are more likely to achieve value for money, efficiency and accountability if they respond to openings identified by the private sector than if they define their own agenda in isolation. However, he also believes that if this is the case, private companies should be made to pay for the service they receive from public institutions.

Other economic characteristics of research which have a bearing on supply should also be noted. First, there may be large economies of scale in research and, second, research may have both positive and negative externalities, especially with regard to longer-term environmental factors. Both these factors militate towards a continued public role.

4.3 Progress towards new goals

Private sector research, especially in Africa, is still in its infancy, though estimates of its importance vary. When they conducted their research in Kenya in the mid-1990s, Beynon and Mbogoh (1996) estimated that the private sector was responsible for approximately 15% of the total agricultural research underway in the country. Pray and Echeverria (1991), on the other hand calculate that the private sector rarely accounts for more than 10% of overall national research expenditures. Although they make no estimate of the percentage of valuable results which this 10% generates, they do emphasise that results are more impressive because of the greater emphasis on linkages (between farmers, researchers and technology transfer agents) in the private sector.

Hobbs and Taylor (1987) concur in this. They believe that private sector research has advantages in being appropriate, having good extension and rapid, painstaking and accurate reporting on all financial expenditures. Antholt (1994) is also a supporter of the private sector. He cites the example of the rubber, tea and coconut research institutes in Sri Lanka which used to be efficient when funded by private industry but since nationalisation, have become far less so. This view concurs with the quite widely-held belief that, though they produce much of value, the overall efficiency of public research systems remains well below what we should be aiming for (hence the continued need for scrutiny and innovation in structures and mechanisms for financing research).

Pray and Echeverria (1990) believe that better linkages between research and marketing in private companies generate more marketable products. As an example they cite two Virginia tobacco breeding programmes in Bangladesh, one public sector and the other run by the private Bangladesh Tobacco Company. The private sector company identified the importance of smoking quality to tobacco acceptability and rigorously tested and measured this during the varietal development process. The public organisation had no testing facilities and, as a result, continued to produce varieties which grew well but had a poor leaf quality, fetched low market prices and, as a consequence, were rarely grown by farmers. This also provides an example of duplication of effort resulting in wasteful use of public resources. A more extreme example of such duplication often takes place at an international level.

Generally speaking national research institutes around the world have paid inadequate attention to the opportunities for 'borrowing' technology. Even the smallest countries have tried to build up research structures which focus most of their efforts on technology generation. Eyzaguirre (1996) argues that small countries should endeavour to become effective 'borrowers' of technology. They should develop systems which enable them effectively to screen the technology options available elsewhere and should put a greater proportion of resources into importing and adapting these, rather than always attempting to 'go it alone'. It should be noted, though, that such a strategy can be considerably complicated if a large proportion of relevant research is conducted within the private sector (which for commercial reasons may be unwilling to share 'results').

One result of diversification of supply in agricultural research is that individual researchers have more choice as to where they will work; indeed there is likely to be competition for human resources (Piñeiro, 1986). This is seen as having a positive impact in terms of the dynamism of the system as a whole. Researchers themselves are considered to be more productive in the private sector as they have greater access to resources (Dalrymple and Srivastava, 1994). However there are drawbacks as well. If all the high quality researchers are working in the private sector, Piñeiro (1986) suggests that this will dangerously erode the public sector support base. Farmers will look elsewhere for solutions to their problems and cease to lobby on behalf of the national research system (this argument presupposes that the farmers have at some time had confidence in the public sector research system which is not always the case). The problem is compounded by the fact that if the public sector focuses on basic research, its results will become increasingly less visible to consumers. Piñeiro's hypothesis is that as agricultural development takes place, further change becomes more dependent upon the use of improved inputs. These will be closely associated with their suppliers who will consequently be seen as the catalysts of such development, regardless of whether initial research findings in fact came from the public institutions. The end result could be a reduction in the capacity of public institutions to perform vital basic, or supporting, research.

This is a problem which Jarvis (1994) identified in Chile. During the fruit boom of the 1970s the Chilean government effectively withdrew from research into export fruits. At that time private companies readily took its place. However, when the boom ended the kind of adaptive research that these private companies had been conducting became less productive, especially since most of the relatively easy gains had already been made. What was required at this stage was a renewed emphasis on basic research but private companies proved unwilling to invest in this area and the government's capacity to do so had severely diminished. According to Jarvis this cycle undermined the overall effectiveness of the Chilean research system.

Decentralisation of public institutions along the lines of Mali's efforts can increase local participation and accountability. Such an approach is particularly important in countries like Israel, where the very distinct agroecological environments in different regions require separate treatment. However, in such cases the emphasis must be on effective communication between different regional institutes to avoid wasteful duplication (Blum, 1991). Also, in isolation, decentralisation will solve few problems. In Mali it was felt necessary to supplement the benefits of the decentralised structure by establishing Research Users' Commissions at both central and regional levels to institutionalise user consultation in the technology generation process (Collion, 1994).

There has, as yet, been little systematic research into the impact of the new competitive technology funds which have been established in many countries. What evidence there is is quite mixed. In Tanzania a National Agricultural Research Fund (ARF) was established under the umbrella of a the World Bank supported National Agriculture and Livestock Research Project in the early 1990s, its aim being to 'provide a transparent mechanism for receiving and disbursing funds.....as part of the implementation of the National Agricultural Research Masterplan' (MoA/Department of Research and Training bulletin on the ARF). The Research Fund was viewed as a 'simple prototype for an eventual Consolidated Funding Mechanism for a sustainable agricultural research system'. Subsidiary objectives included, *inter alia*: the establishment of linkages between various national and international research institutions; the promotion of cost effective research to improve the research environment within the government service; and the facilitation of the acquisition and administration of funds provided by the private sector, donor organisations and the GoT. It is notable that increasing the client-orientation of research was not mentioned as a key objective of the original ARF.

The fund was initially intended to cover both research and research-related activities (such as travel grants and honoraria for visiting scientists and dissertation work for young scientists) though a decision was subsequently taken to delay its use for the latter purposes. It was managed day-to-day by a small secretariat (chief administrative officer, secretary and finance officer) based at the Department of Research and Training's (DRT's) Dar es Salaam headquarters. Governance was through a 12 member Management team comprising representatives from DRT (the Commissioner and two Assistant Commissioners); the two national universities; the extension services; the private sector (a bank and the Tanzania Farmers' Association); other public sector organisations; and donors (the FAO representative). A detailed list of eligible topics for research was drawn up and circulated, together with basic instructions on submission of proposals. Proposals were assessed by a peer review panel and recommendations on funding made to the Management team.

The NALRP experience with this research fund was, by almost universal agreement, well below expectations. Problems cited included (from the perspective of potential applicants): inadequate publicity given to the existence of the fund; confusion over mechanisms for application; and slow and *ad hoc* procedures for application (apparently even when projects had been agreed, funds were very slow to be released). From the fund management side there was a belief that: proposals submitted were below standard; researchers did not like being subjected to new and stringent quality standards; financial/disbursement technicalities delayed the start; and delays were due to a slow project review process. Other commentators mentioned undue bureaucracy and the possibility of corrupt practices. As a result, disbursements under the fund have been well below expectations (Carney, 1997).

The Agricultural Research Fund established in Kenya in 1990 has been considerably more successful, though it too had teething problems, as did a similar fund in Ghana. Part of the trouble has been that researchers from national agricultural research institutes have resented the loss of resources and power implied by the move to 'open' fund financing. These researchers must now compete where formerly they had a near monopoly of research resources within the formal system. Indeed, in the case of Kenya, researchers from the Kenya Agricultural Research Institute (KARI) were initially not eligible to apply for fund resources at all, though the fund was managed through KARI systems (this ruling has now been changed as the fund moves into its second cycle). Any active resistance or delaying tactics by researchers or research administrators can clearly reduce the efficiency gains generated by the move to competitive financing.

The prospects for enhancing accountability through competitive research funds are, however, significant. The committees and boards which manage the funds are usually drawn from a range of stakeholder groups. Nevertheless, there remains a considerable way to go on this front. In the early stages those who sit on such committees are usually quite removed from the day to day realities of farmers' livelihoods. It is only after significant capacity-building that representatives from bodies which are closer to resource-poor farmers can make an active contribution to these committees, and thus to the overall accountability of the research system.

4.4 Focus on the rural poor

Once more, by not being in a position to purchase the technology which is generated by private sector research, the poor have gained less than the relatively better off farmers from diversification in the supply of agricultural research. Commodity boards tend to deal with export crops which are often less important to the poor than food crops and NGO research efforts are not generally broad in their coverage (though those poor living in villages receiving intensive support have certainly gained). The issue of trends in overall research spending in developing countries is not addressed by the literature covered here, and thus the extent to which private research adds to, rather than substitutes for, public research is unclear.

On the other hand, even if the poor do not benefit immediately from the new pluralism within the research system they are likely to benefit from overall increases in the supply of agricultural research in the longer term. (If private research organisations are more productive than their public sector counterparts, as most commentators argue, then the stock of research results will increase even if overall expenditure on research remains static). The price of new products (the product of research) frequently falls over time as manufacturing techniques improve and competition in supply increases. Non-paying farmers can also benefit from spillovers: information which forms part of new product packages may prove to have broader applicability to a wider range of people than those for whom it was originally developed or those who were the first to 'purchase' it. Sutherland et al. (1998), for example, note that livestock research on a DFID funded project in Kenya did not benefit the poorest farmers at the outset but since these people were employed as day labourers for richer farmers they were soon exposed to the new technologies (e.g. for mange control) which they could then adapt to their own circumstances and selectively adopt.

Finally, changes in the supply of research have been coupled with an overall effort to enhance the responsiveness of all research to the needs of the rural poor. ISNAR studies show that this has been extremely difficult to achieve (Merrill-Sands and Kaimowitz, 1991), but certainly this is becoming an increasing focus of attention in many public research institutes, especially those which have received donor support. There has been much attention paid to using participatory techniques to facilitate the involvement of resource poor farmers in the technology generation and transfer process. Various group approaches, ranging from specialised research groups established by public sector organisations to self-sustaining groups of farmers who interact with research institutions on their own terms, have been tried. In addition new agricultural research funds are attempting to use structural methods to ensure responsiveness to the needs of the poor (stipulating that research will only be financed if there is clear evidence that it is demanded by poor farmers).

It must be said, however, that none of these approaches fully solves the problem of representation of the interests of the very poorest farmers. These people are usually unable to spare the time and resources to take part in research groups and are often not members of self sustaining farmers' organisations (because of entry barriers including annual fees). Even where they are members of such organisations or where their interests are supposed to be directly represented (for example on the committees that govern the allocation of agricultural research funds) it is usually the case that this representation is inadequate (Pijnenburg, 1998; Collion and Rondot, 1998; Carney, 1996). Committees which deal with research issues often face a dilemma; they wish to include representatives of the 'poorest' but places are limited and they need to ensure that all committee members will contribute to the discussion.

It is rare to find farmers who remain close to the grass roots yet have the capacity to participate as full partners in technology committees. Indeed, many of the poorest farmers are either unaware of the existence of agricultural research organisations or at least unaware of what it is that they actually do. Considerable capacity building with potential representatives is therefore required before the views of the poorest can gain equal voice with the views of scientists and richer, more well-educated and articulate farmers.

4.5 Lessons

Most authors follow Pray and Echeverria (1991) in asserting that there are a range of different reasons for government intervention in agricultural research. Evenson and David (1993) argue that in the rice sector passive reliance on the private sector would not have generated anything like the technology improvements which have been witnessed over the last thirty years. They also emphasise that rice research and extension must be guided by 'informed public policy discussion'. Similarly, many commentators highlight the fact that the Green Revolution in south and south east Asia, equivalent gains in maize productivity in Zimbabwe and other sub-Saharan African countries, and the dramatic gains in temperate country yields have all been underpinned by public sector investment, particularly during their early phases.

Nevertheless, there is increasing evidence that the private sector will become involved at multiple points within the agricultural technology system if given the chance. There is also a good deal of conjecture that the public sector, and donors in particular, may already have crowded out viable private sector investment in technology development. However, there is no strong evidence to suggest that the private sector will supply and extend technology and the products in which it is embedded (e.g. seeds) at anything like *optimal* levels (in terms of aggregate food supply and poverty reduction considerations) without additional support (Byerlee, 1996). Obviously this is more true the more public characteristics are exhibited by the technology or item in question. There are, though, also questions of trading risks, credit and information availability and profit to be taken into consideration.

Of all the sub-sectors addressed in this review, it is probably in the area of agricultural research (and perhaps extension) that the highest level of disquiet remains about whether the most appropriate way forward has been identified. Few dispute the need for continued agricultural research. Now that we have largely exhausted the supply of new land which can be profitably and sustainably brought into agricultural production, there is little else to fall back upon to meet the rising demand for food than research into yield enhancing technologies and practices (Crosson and Anderson, 1994). It has been estimated that sub-Saharan Africa as a whole requires an agricultural growth rate of 4% per annum (twice the growth rate of the past three decades) if nutritional levels are to improve significantly. To make this possible, 3.5% of the growth will need to derive from yield increases with only 0.5% per annum coming from increases in cropped area (Larson and Frisvold, 1996).

However an equally small number of people would be likely to claim that we have identified 'the best way forward' in agricultural technology development and transfer. It is clear that the public sector must continue to play an important role but the history of public sector involvement in research is littered with wastage, lack of relevance and failure. It is for this reason that increasing attention is being paid to designing and developing alternative structures through which research can be conducted, notably partnerships financed through accountable grants and user-controlled funds (Alex, 1997). Perhaps the key lesson that we should learn is that we must continue to innovate in this area, to monitor closely the progress of innovations and to keep the varied needs of poor farmers at the forefront of our minds when designing the parameters of or executing any change.

5. Agricultural extension systems

5.1 Changes in supply or supplier
In many people's minds extension and government are indissolubly linked. Yet elements of privatisation and diversification in supply of extension services have been witnessed throughout the world over the past two decades. Developed countries such as Britain and France have made enormous steps towards complete privatisation of their services and other countries as ideologically diverse as Chile and China have moved to new contractual extension arrangements. The new characterisation is of a 'pluralistic' service drawing on a variety of different bodies all with different strengths and objectives.

In some countries, particularly in Latin America, the private and non-governmental sectors have been actively brought in by the government. Antholt (1994) argues that in Asia, on the other hand, this has not happened, even when the importance of the private sector has been recognised. Active encouragement of non-governmental participants is most effective when the government is willing to retain responsibility for a large part of the cost of the service, at least while the new providers are getting established (this is tantamount to infant industry protection). In practice this means that governments stipulate a period over which they will finance extension services but subcontract actual delivery. For example the National Extension Service (NES) in Zaire invited local NGOs and private cotton companies to provide extension in their local areas. NES provided training, equipment, funding and monitoring.

Most of the clearest examples of this type of government policy are drawn from Latin America, where both private trade and civil organisations are more developed. In Costa Rica the World Bank is supporting a project in which farmers are allocated vouchers which they can then use to contract in private extension services. The government trains the new extension agents and aims to phase out vouchers after seven years, leaving farmers to make direct payments to private agents (Ameur, 1994).

Chile's first attempt at privatisation, the replacement in the early 1980s of the Agricultural Extension Service by a Private Technical Assistance scheme, failed because of the 'false assumption that there is a market of technical assistance in the rural areas of Chile' and because of widespread fraud (Berdegué, 1994 & 1997)). After this experience a more gradualist approach was taken. In 1986 the Agricultural Development Institute of the Ministry of Agriculture (INDAP) introduced subsidised private consulting services for smaller farmers and drew up a plan to discontinue public services to medium and large farmers. Those farmers who remain eligible for public services are assessed and grouped according to their access to resources and their productive potential. The poorest ones become the beneficiaries of a scheme which has a primarily social emphasis (PTTB) and for which they make no financial contributions (although a 15% contribution is planned). Better endowed farmers are catered to by a more market-oriented scheme (PTTI). This focuses on commercial development and incorporates increasing farmer contributions over the years. In both cases farmers receive services as members of groups rather than as individuals. Firms and NGOs seek certification by INDAP to allow them to bid for contracts to provide extension services – and other services such as credit provision and rural youth programmes – in a particular area (Berdegué, 1997). The recipients themselves draw up a medium term agricultural development plan for their locality, with the assistance of private consultants who are hired directly by INDAP. By October 1995 there were 139 TTCs (technology transfer consultancies) registered by INDAP. Berdegué (1997) reports the breakdown by coverage of these TTCs to be: 40% of clients serviced by private commercial companies, 36% by NGOs, 17% by farmer organisations and 7% by universities, municipal governments etc.

The Chilean system is now in a situation of 'permanent innovations' (Berdegué, 1997). The public sector has almost entirely withdrawn from direct provision and increasingly farmers themselves are contributing to the costs of extension. In 1995 only 30% of the 50,000 farm households which benefit from the scheme were making no financial contribution. The remainder were paying between US$12.5 and US$62.5 per year. As of 1996 all farmers were expected to make a contribution. Recovery rates for these amounts were, in 1995, reported to be at least 75%. The state is in transition from being a provider of services to a regulator while 'beneficiaries' gradually change to become 'clients'. A further change is that INDAP is increasingly providing not just technical services but also financial services, agribusiness advice and support to organisational development.

In both Chile and Costa Rica new providers (private agents) are combined with new sources of financing – the beneficiaries themselves. However, cost recovery from beneficiaries can take place without a change in the physical supplier of services. This has been the case under a World Bank project in Mexico where the public sector still supplies the services. Once again, farmers are stratified according to wealth and those in the richer, irrigated areas must pay up to 50% of the costs of extension services and 100% for personalised services such as soil sampling and animal feed mix formulation. After a three year period of intensive services, the level of provision is reduced unless farmers wish to take on the whole cost of intensive services themselves (Wilson, 1991). This project is also experimenting with cost cutting measures through innovative methods such as increased use of information technology (Umali and Schwartz, 1994).

Under a decentralisation programme in Colombia the federal government is withdrawing from extension provision, including financing, in favour of the municipalities. These must pay for services out of local taxes with central government providing cofinancing through an Integrated Rural Development Fund. Instead of providing actual services, the role of the Colombian Agricultural and Livestock Institute is now to train both private and public extension agents employed by the municipalities (Wilson, 1991). Though government employees, the activities of these agents are supposed to be overseen by a Municipal Rural Development Council

(MRDC) in which farmers hold a majority of seats. The success of these MRDCs seems, though, to be in some doubt (Berdegué, 1997).

Perhaps the most notable model of decentralisation and mixed public/private services comes from China. There, groups of farmers sign contracts for the provision of extension advice with Agrotechnical Extension Centres (which operate all the way from the national to the township level) as well as research institutes, universities and individuals (Ameur, 1994). Since liberalisation began in 1978 farmers' organisations have begun to spring up throughout China. These receive technical advice from a number of sources, notably through scientists and others who are invited to sit on their boards and become 'shareholders' in what are usually market-based enterprises (CECAT/RCRE, 1996).

Although the most prominent examples of changes in supply of extension services come from Latin America, progress in this direction has also been made in Africa and elsewhere. A key development has been the acceptance by the World Bank within its numerous extension support programmes that other players (that is others beyond the national extension service) have a role to play in extension. The World Bank's original Training and Visit (T&V) extension programmes were based on the notion of a public sector monopoly whereas now the role of farmers' organisations, NGOs and the private sector is explicitly recognised and sometimes directly supported (Collion and Rondot, 1998).

Perhaps the most impressive example of a farmer-driven service which offers a full alternative to the public sector is that established by the Uganda National Farmers' Association (UNFA). UNFA, with assistance from Danida, has established a 'demand-driven, cost-recovery' extension service in a number of Districts in Uganda. Members of the organisation request training or advice on a particular topic and this is provided by UNFA employees who charge a fee to all beneficiaries. The success of the scheme has varied from District to District but in some places demand has been very high and UNFA has been forced to expand its numbers of technical personnel. Many of these UNFA extension agents are former public sector extension agents and so are well connected with existing service networks which is obviously a considerable advantage (Olsen, 1996). The apparent success of the scheme is such that UNFA has been requested to take over general extension provision from the District government in at least one District (the decentralisation programme in Uganda has put extension in the hands of the Districts; the future of the national extension body is now being reviewed).

Private sector involvement in extension is not, however, limited to taking over the functions formerly performed by public sector institutions. Schwartz (1994) and Umali and Schwartz (1994) list numerous different forms of extension by private companies. The most simple is when private input supply companies – often the same companies that were discussed in the previous sections on seeds, research and fertiliser – provide information with their products. This they do in the interests of marketing their own products. Some development projects are also beginning to recognise the potential of working with traders to deliver information, as traders are in regular contact with farmers and have existing networks (Compton, 1997).

Schwartz (1994) notes that private extension is generally not a stand-alone activity but will be provided where three conditions hold. First, purchased inputs must be necessary to achieve desired production results. Second, these purchased inputs must be cost effective relative to output prices. Third, there should be a fairly high degree of competition between input suppliers for the same market share. This latter condition is probably too extreme in that potential competition could be just as good a catalyst to the provision of product advice as actual competition.

Private sector extension may be provided not only by companies wishing to sell to farmers, but also by those wishing to purchase from them. As Schwartz (1994) notes, extension advice may be provided both to increase product quality to the benefit of the purchaser and as a way to promote partnership with suppliers. This latter point is important especially where several firms are competing to purchase the same produce. In Kenya private companies have introduced new technology for producing high quality horticultural goods. In order to benefit from the investment that they have made in research and providing advice, they must ensure that the farmers sell to them. Thus they often have to expend resources on 'policing' so that produce is not 'poached' (Schwartz, 1994). Any loyalty-building extension advice can reduce the need to do this.

Both motives (i.e. increasing quality and enhancing partnership) are apparent in the provision of extension advice in the dairy sector in Argentina. A recession there in the mid 1970s made other types of agriculture relatively more attractive to farmers. Threatened with a loss of raw materials, two dairy plants, the cooperative SANCOR (Santa-Fe Cordoba United Cooperatives) and a private company, La Serenissima, moved into dairy development. SANCOR established an extension and artificial insemination service for cooperatives and small groups of farmers. La Serenissima targeted medium and large scale farmers with media broadcasts and publications through five regional offices with over one hundred professional staff. Both efforts resulted in significant increases in the amount of milk delivered (Umali et al., 1992).

Groups of companies, in the form of producer associations, can also provide extension advice. Such associations act, in some ways, as publicity arms for their members and as such they tend to be more ready than individual firms to engage in activities without immediate commercial benefits. In Zimbabwe the Agro-chemical Industry Association has a safety programme which tries to find packages of protective clothing which are more affordable for small farmers and in India the Fertiliser Association publishes literature and has set up hundreds of demonstration plots (Umali and Schwartz, 1994).

However, as in research, it is not just private companies which are moving to supply extension services. Individuals within the government extension services may supply advice on a private basis. For example in Ecuador extension agents effectively sharecrop with farmers. They provide advice and inputs (which they are able to secure on credit with the guarantee of their government salaries) while the farmers supply land and labour (Wilson, 1991; Umali and Schwartz, 1994). Unlicensed individuals outside the public sector can also provide advice. Ameur (1994) reports that this is common in China.

In addition, commodity organisations, NGOs and groups of farmers are also formal suppliers of extension services. The first of these, commodity organisations, have been a significant force in extending new production techniques. For example, in the early 1980s the Malaysia Rubber Industries Smallholders Development Authority provided extension advice to more than half a million smallholders through about 1,500 extension agents, financed by smallholders' production contributions (Maalouf et al., 1991).

In rural areas, especially those which can be classified as complex, diverse and risk-prone where many farmers cannot afford to buy advice and government services are often very weak, NGOs may be the main providers of extension services. Not only do they provide the services themselves but they are also responsible for developing many of the methodologies for research and extension work which are subsequently adopted by the public sector (Farrington and Amanor, 1991).

Farmers' organisations may be both consumers and providers of information and extension services (Umali and Schwartz, 1994). Larger, more formal organisations, such as the Argentine Association of Agricultural Experimentation Groups (AACREA) and UNFA (mentioned above), tend to provide more advice than they consume. They are financed to do so either by membership dues – $60 per month in the Argentine case – or, in the case of the El Ceibo cocoa cooperative in Bolivia, through a combination of product revenues (a percentage of annual profits and sales revenues), NGO and donor funding. El Ceibo provides both agronomic advice and training in business methods and general education to its members (Schwartz, 1994; Bebbington et al., 1996). Smaller organisations are more likely to consume advice, though they might also generate and share information internally.

It should be noted, however, that farmers' organisations tend to be less involved in technology generation and transfer activities than many have assumed. There are a number of reasons for this, the most important being: lack of both financial and human resources; the complexity and diversity of members' needs – especially when members produce a variety of different crops under different production conditions; farmers' organisations' lack of familiarity with the processes and institutions involved in the formal technology generation and transfer system; and the fact that members often do not prioritise this area of involvement, (it is common to find that they are more interested in immediate issues such as market access and prices) (Carney, 1996; Collion and Rondot, 1998).

5.2 Economic analysis

The characterisation of extension as either a public or a private good depends both upon the nature of the extension itself and also upon the stage of development of the country in question. While Leonard (1985) argues that 'most extension work is inevitably a public good everywhere in the world', Wilson (1991) believes that information on new technology is a public good but that as a certain level of technology becomes widely accepted extension becomes a private good. At this stage farmers require a more individually tailored problem solving service – such information will be subtractable and excludable and, so long as it is high quality, they should be willing to pay for it.

Umali and Schwartz (1994) concur in this view over the long term. They see general agricultural information, designed to improve existing cultural and production practices, as a toll good in the short term. It is not subtractable in that one person's use of the information does not reduce its availability for others, but it is excludable; not all farmers receive the information at the same time – indeed the speed of information dissemination can vary enormously, partly due to differences in medium (word of mouth versus mass media for example) and differences in quality of the communications infrastructure. In the long term, however, Umali and Schwartz (1994) believe that information is diffusive and therefore will no longer be excludable, rendering it a public good. At this stage it is ineligible for private supply except by purchasing companies which themselves benefit from increasing the speed of information dissemination or as a 'secondary task' which complements another activity. This possibility is emphasised by Schwartz (1994). She notes that some extension information, despite being a public good, only benefits those who have access to certain inputs, facilities or credit. The public sector can therefore cut back on its costs by leaving the provision of this type of information to the private sector.

It is only by making information 'specialised' that it becomes excludable for the duration which, in turn, reduces the need for public sector intervention in the market. Specialised information will either not be relevant to other farmers, as is the case with the information generated by soil analysis, or, like marketing information, it will be so valuable to them that they will not wish to share it (Umali and Schwartz, 1994).

The stage of development of a country has a bearing not only on the prevailing levels of technology but also on the demand for agricultural produce and the difficulty of providing extension (Umali and Schwartz, 1994). It can be argued that in countries with a shortage of basic food crops, governments should do everything in their power to raise aggregate production and thus provision of all types of information should remain in their hands. Indeed Wilson (1991) argues that most technology for basic food crops will always remain a public good and therefore should be provided by the public sector. The implication here is that narrow goals of economic efficiency are replaced by a broader aim of enhancing general welfare in a country. Extension programmes with this and other types of social goals will always require public funding. The difficult task will be to take decisions as to their scope. These decisions will have to be based not on an assessment of economic characteristics but on social priorities.

The question then becomes whether extension is an effective tool for increasing social welfare. Beynon and Duncan (1996) and Alston and Pardey (1996) are sceptical of the merits of technology spending in this regard (this would include both research and extension). Both sets of authors view such spending as a 'blunt instrument' for addressing equity considerations. Alston and Pardey go into some detail about the tradeoffs between equity and efficiency in research spending; their discussion illustrates how little systematic attention has been paid to this matter and how much more work there is to be done. Beynon and Duncan (1996) are particularly concerned with extension and the use of this as a mechanism to reduce poverty in rural areas. They argue that it would be better to place extension on a more commercial footing and to seek alternative means to support for rural people and their livelihoods.

Even if efficiency is the primary aim, some market intervention may be necessary because of the existence of imperfections due to the 'lumpy' nature of extension advice and adverse selection (Smith and Thomson, 1991). The first problem concerns that fact that marketed information is usually sold at the same cost to all farmers, regardless of the size of their operation. This means that the cost per unit of output is far higher for smaller than for larger farmers. Indeed information sold to small farmers may even be charged at a higher absolute rate because of the greater costs associated with serving those with lower levels of education in more distant areas (two common attributes of smaller farmers). The formation of farmers' organisations to act as purchasing consortia is one response to this problem. If this is the primary reason why a farmers' organisation is formed it would support the view expressed in World Bank (1994b) that relevant advice, by definition, has an attractive cost:benefit ratio and therefore should be saleable, in some shape or form.

Finally, the problem of adverse selection occurs because private extension providers (and public ones too) may knowingly provide erroneous information. The perceived threat of this might reduce consumption to sub-optimal levels (Umali and Schwartz, 1994). This problem might be particularly acute in the extension sector because farmers are unaccustomed to paying for information and they may, therefore, have serious problems with valuation. The difficulty for governments which hope to regulate is that they may be in no better position to value the information than farmers themselves – especially if they have withdrawn entirely from providing services or conducting research in the area in question. In this case the costs of regulation might exceed the benefits, a possibility raised by Smith and Thomson (1991).

5.3 Progress towards new goals

Changes in extension, perhaps more than in other areas, seem to be due to governments' own recognition of the financial insustainability or general inadequacy of their services. Antholt (1994) cites the example of the 1990-1 Tamil Nadu extension budget. Salaries accounted for 88% of total spending and only $1 per extension agent was allocated for 'materials and supplies'. The possibility of providing an effective service was essentially ruled out at the budgetary stage.

Donor pressure to reform systems which, despite their own involvement, they see as unresponsive to farmers' needs and financially problematic, has also been strong. A recent World Bank evaluation of completed extension projects, all of which were located within and designed to help the public sector, shows that 90% have experienced recurrent-cost funding problems and 70% are probably not sustainable. In 84% of the projects research-extension linkages were considered inadequate to ensure that the needs of some of the major farming systems were defined and addressed and just over 50% demonstrated an entrenched 'top-down' approach in developing recommendations, despite objectives of continuous feedback from farmers (World Bank, 1994b). An important new recommendation by the Operations Evaluation Department of the World Bank is that 'some Bank departments may have to modify their traditional approach of installing (or continuing to support) relatively uniform national programs regardless of local circumstances' (Purcell and Anderson, 1997). This suggests that the Bank has recognised the diversity of conditions which obtain within developing countries and recognised the problems associated with centrally designed extension structures.

Non-traditional suppliers of extension would seem to have little to live up to, although it is questionable whether the 'lean teams' of private extension agents postulated by Ameur (1994) are actually forthcoming in developing countries. Antholt (1991) argues that the single most important thing in an extension service is control by beneficiaries. He develops this thesis in Antholt (1994) into an argument that beneficiaries should bear at least some of the cost of the service, for the following three reasons. First, this gives ownership and drawing rights on the services. Second, it takes some financial pressure off the government, thereby increasing the chances of sustainability and third, it provides the basis for a more demand-driven, responsive and accountable service.

Thus, for him, all private services and government cost recovery systems are by definition more efficient and more accountable than their predecessors. They are also better at responding to farmers' needs. He does, however, note that the degree to which this is true depends upon certain other factors such as farmer participation, professional competence of extension agents (seen as a 'major constraint' in nearly all free-standing World Bank projects, Purcell and Anderson (1997)) and cost effectiveness. It is probably safe to say that private or NGO services could not be worse than many public sector suppliers in these respects – and with competition they will surely be better. A glowing example of all these qualities seems to be provided by the extension agents in China who sign contracts directly with farmers in highly competitive environments and whose payments are based upon farmer performance (Umali and Schwartz, 1994).

However, unless public sector cost recovery is accompanied by increased competition, improvements in cost effectiveness may be slow to materialise. Indeed Antholt (1994) argues that public sector services are always isolated and slow to adapt. It is Wilson (1991) and Rivera and Gustafson (1991), however, who point out some of the operational difficulties with cost recovery programmes, such as defining the criteria upon which charges are made and actually collecting the payments. Ingram (1992) points out one of the first operational implications of implementing cost recovery schemes in the UK: civil servants needed new skills – they particularly required training in marketing techniques.

In Chile, as of May 1997, demand for services is identified by local groups, government authorities or INDAP staff. A 'cooperation agreement' which lays out rights and responsibilities on each side is signed between the local group and INDAP. After a process of bidding, a contract is signed between the service provider and INDAP (acting on behalf of farmers) or, more recently, the farmers' group itself. The work plan for service provision is agreed in advance for a period of 3–5 years; INDAP undertakes to monitor progress through specially hired consultants, though recently the client group itself has become more involved in evaluating the service it has received. Payments by INDAP are made on the basis of performance (fines are levied for poor performance). Recently it has been agreed that the client group will be able to terminate its contract with the service providing agency at any time if performance falls below expectations. As it is, those organisations which are rated to have provided the 'worst' service through the year are replaced as a matter of course (Berdegué, 1997). It is clear that this system is strongly oriented towards increasing the overall quality of extension services in Chile, including improving effectiveness, accountability and efficiency. Indeed, Berdegué (1997) notes that 'there is no doubt that [the new system] is significantly more cost effective than a public alternative would be, that a larger fraction of the total cost can be used to pay for field-level activities rather than for fixed office-level expenses, and that through a number of progressive improvements the system has become much more cost effective than at the beginning'. It is, however, only now (1997–8) that a full scale evaluation of the system as a whole is being conducted.

Rivera and Gustafson (1991) emphasise that, whatever benefits accrue from public sector cost recovery, 'public sector extension alone will never attend the entire demand for extension services by the world's farmers'. Schwartz concurs in this. She argues that 'the existence of multiple (sometimes conflicting) information sources is an advantage for farmers in that they can best select the information mix most suited to their goals as producers and the most reliable information source' (Schwartz, 1994). The argument is that extending the choice available to farmers is a good in its own right. Consequently not just public sector cost recovery but also the replacement of a government monopoly with a private monopoly in a certain area (which is effectively what happens for short periods in Chile, despite competitive bidding) is very much a second best option for reform. Decentralisation of government efforts also falls into this category if it creates a system of local monopolies. This may be one of the problems with the Colombian system, which is also criticised for undue politicisation (Berdegué, 1997).

One other factor which may help private extension agents provide a more effective service is their closeness to product markets. They are far better able than government or NGOs to feed marketing information into the extension process (Hobbs and Taylor, 1987). Indeed this is the driving force behind purchasing company information dissemination. An example of this is also provided by the El Ceibo cocoa cooperative in Bolivia which identified the market opportunities in organic cocoa and then begun research and extension work to try to address some of the problems raised by this type of cultivation (Healy, 1987; Bebbington et al., 1996). Hercus (1991) argues that the commercialisation of advisory services in New Zealand has forced those offering the services to look more closely at the farm in its environment, producing as part of a commercial system rather than as an isolated production maximiser.

The final issue that should be borne in mind, however, is that in some areas there simply may not be any relevant technology to extend. The World Bank (1994b) criticises the projects it reviews for having always assumed that such technology was available. If no relevant technology is available a change in service provider can logically do nothing to increase the effectiveness of extension. It is NGOs rather than private providers who are likely to be the new entrants in areas where technology is lacking (because these areas are also likely to be very poor). They therefore need to be aware of this possibility and focus their efforts accordingly (perhaps on adaptive research rather than extension in the first instance).

One potential danger that must be averted is that increased pluralism in extension providers further fragments any potential 'demand' that extension might exert on research. Research/extension linkages have been a notoriously problematic area for many years. The theory that extension will feed back farmers' priorities to research seldom seems to hold true in practice (hence the need for researchers themselves to go on-farm). However, this notion should not be entirely abandoned, otherwise the knowledge and experience of extension agents will always remain underutilised. When numerous different types of organisation are involved in extension there is, nonetheless, a clear danger that any systematic links between the two sides will be neglected because of the increased complexity of bringing all sides together.

5.4 Focus on the rural poor

The World Bank (1994b), in emphasising the importance of clients of extension services contributing to their costs, does explicitly recognise the difficulty of this in very poor areas. Its suggestion, which it does not fully develop, is that farmers may make contributions in 'non-cash' terms (presumably labour, attendance at meetings etc.), so that the accountability link is maintained. This would also help to overcome the problem that a number of authors mention of information being deemed less valuable if it is provided for free. The same point is made by Purcell and Anderson (1997) who state that: 'some form of farmer ownership of services should be the ultimate objective, regardless of resource circumstances'.

Unlike in most of the sectors addressed in this review, the extension area provides specific examples, such as those from Chile and Mexico, of a refocusing of government efforts on the poorest sectors of the population. In addition, participatory diagnosis techniques, developed by NGOs in an effort to make planning more responsive to the needs of the poorest, are increasingly being incorporated into public sector activities (Hagmann et al., 1998). The chances of poorer sections of the rural population having benefited from reform in this sub-sector are therefore correspondingly higher than in other areas. Nevertheless, extension services are still plagued with problems in many countries and the extent to which the poor might have benefited should not be over-stated. Reform within large public sector extension services takes a long time and requires constant efforts by those with vision and the leverage to stimulate change. Berdegué (1997) notes that the new systems in Chile seem to be working best with those who are less poor, suggesting that even when the poor are specifically catered for there are significant problems in meeting their needs.

Alternative providers sometimes focus on the poor but a number of the producers' organisations which are providing advice certainly do not reach the poorest farmers. The cost of membership of such organisations can be quite steep. For example, overall costs of membership of the Uganda National Farmers' Association in the first year of joining can be up to US$15–US$20; extension advice must be paid for on top of this. This necessarily makes the organisation somewhat elitist.

Perhaps a key remaining question relates to the extent to which the provision of technical advice is a priority for the poorest groups of rural people. Many of these people do not themselves own land or are not able to adopt new technologies because of the requirements for purchased inputs. One suggestion that has been made is that field extension agents should become far more generalist. In their position as perhaps the only representative of the public sector in rural areas, they should act as a point of contact for local people on matters as diverse as credit, marketing, transport and the traditional technical subjects of extension. Rather than providing advice in all these areas they would act as link people or 'vectors' pointing enquirers in the right direction, to the appropriate department or individual (Christoplos, 1996). To an extent this is what extension agents in developed countries do. They act often as advisers on management issues and help farmers to complete the forms that are required to secure government grants and subsidies, rather than providing them with technical support *per se*. Similar directions seem to be emerging in Peru where local communities are being provided with matching funds which they can then use to commission outside support in areas of their choice. Berdegué (1997) reports that demands from the communities are diversifying into non-agricultural areas such as small-scale agroindustries, traditional handicrafts, aquaculture and marketing. This range of needs presumably reflects the diversity of rural livelihoods in Peru.

Another 'new' direction for extension which might be of benefit to the poor is the increased use of mass media (TV and radio) for the delivery of extension advice. The advantage of such delivery methods is that they are cheap and they enable the public sector to continue to provide a basic service to all farmers which they would not be able to do were they to have to continue to rely on expensive, face to face methods. On the other hand, the poorest are less likely to have radios and televisions themselves. This is where 'listening groups' and the sharing of radios etc. is likely to be important. Further investigation of the scope for such new methods is currently being undertaken in the UK by the University of Reading.

5.5 Lessons

All authors agree that there will always remain a role for the public sector in extension. None, however, argue that a public sector monopoly is an appropriate solution to the numerous and long-debated problems of extension provision (World Bank, 1994b). Antholt (1994) calls for institutional pluralism and lists all the other actors with a role to play in the sector, namely: NGOs, seed companies, implement dealers, fertiliser distributors, TV and radio systems, farmer associations, youth groups, local communities and primary school systems. To make such a system function, governments, and others need a 'broader conceptual vision of extension'.

According to Rivera and Gustafson (1991) extension programmes are 'long-term actions implemented by a network of institutions'. They are extremely complex and because of this complexity, the role of government agents might need to expand rather than contract. Public extension planners should coordinate and attend those needs not supported by the private sector, arbitrate when there is conflicting information, assure accountability of all services to the public and facilitate the operation of the entire complex through regulation and provision of information. These are certainly heavy responsibilities, but the government's role is not simply to act as monitor and provider of last resort. It will also want to plan and implement national agricultural development strategies which may become more difficult in a newly pluralistic environment.

There will therefore be a need for further skills development within the public sector, particularly helping managers to understand their new responsibilities and to project a vision of the revised public sector role in the new environment. At the level of field workers and intermediate managers it will be important not only to offer training in new skills (for example social mobilisation and participatory rural appraisal techniques) but also to focus on improving these people's immediate working environments. Tendler (1997) points out that if field extension workers operate in an environment which encourages responsiveness and in which they are encouraged to take their own initiatives, even public sector services can be highly effective. (In north east Brasil she finds the public services which have these characteristics to be more effective than parallel private services in which workers are not so facilitated in performing their tasks). A key first step is to understand local knowledge networks and to build on these, rather than to attempt to deplace them.

A key reason why it is important to devise a coherent public sector policy on extension is that the extent to which other bodies will be willing to provide extension services is partially determined by government actions. Umali and Schwartz (1994) note the particular influence of commodity prices (in turn dependent upon price, trade, fiscal, monetary and exchange rate policy), the degree of development of the supporting infrastructure and the level of education of farmers (this affects both their absorptive capacity and their ability to access cheaper written and broadcast extension materials), amongst other things. All these are influenced by government policy as are farmers' security of tenure and, often, access to credit which can be important determinants of demand for extension services.

Given the arguments in section (c) above about the overall increases in efficiency and accountability which attend diversification and competition in supply of extension services, the main emphasis of government policy should therefore be to enhance the enabling environment for non-governmental provision of extension services. This will include using its limited resources and influence to support forums in which all players (including supporting research organisations) can come together to share experience and plan a future in which rural people's needs are more efficiently serviced on a sustainable basis.

6. Veterinary services

6.1 Changes in supply or supplier

In developed countries it has long been the case that veterinary services are provided on a private, consumer-pays basis. However, in most developing countries such services were freely provided by the public sector from colonial times. Since the inception of such services, however, the livestock population of most countries has grown enormously. Government budgets have not kept pace and services have deteriorated.

While in the research and extension areas the problem has often been an inability or unwillingness on the part of government agencies to identify the needs of the rural poor, in the provision of veterinary services the main issue has been a lack of funds and hence of a broad, effective service. Hence the emphasis in recent years has been on cost recovery in the public service, coupled with complementary private services in some countries. Indeed in their survey of twenty nine African countries and eight Asian and Latin American countries Umali et al. (1992) show that by 1991 no country offered completely free veterinary services. Even in the three main animal health areas, namely clinical care, delivery of vaccinations and vector control (as opposed to the provision of drugs or artificial insemination) all operated either full cost recovery schemes or a combination, including subsidies, rather than entirely cost free provision.

When NGOs – such as Proshika in Bangladesh, Intermediate Technology in Kenya and India and BAIF in India – have been involved their role has largely been to extend services to regions which were formally unreached, often through training paravets or members of the community (Khan et al., 1991; Grandin et al., 1991). There has been much debate over the most suitable roles and responsibilities for such paraprofessionals (Holden et al., 1996, FAO Email conference on Principles for Rational Delivery of Public and Private Veterinary Services, 1997). There are essentially two models: the first is to train members of the community to provide basic animal health advice; the second is to develop a cadre of paravets with lower levels of training and lower income expectations than fully-fledged veterinarians. Such paravets are particularly suited to areas with high levels of poultry and small ruminant production as for these animals routine preventative work tends to be more important than diagnostic services. Given the poor quality of infrastructure and large distances which must be covered in many of the more remote area it is important to equip paravets simultaneously to provide both animal health and animal production advice as well as marketing advice (where possible).

Farmers' organisations have also made efforts to improve services to their members. One mechanism for achieving this has been to organise routes which public veterinarians follow on specified days, enabling members to gather to receive services (Leonard, 1993; Umali et al., 1992). Another has been to employ veterinarians themselves (Gros, 1994). One of the largest scale efforts by a farmers' association has been in the Central African Republic where the National Federation of Livestock Producers (FNEC), with donor assistance, successfully undertook the distribution of veterinary drugs after the collapse of the public system in 1973. Following this it expanded its activities and scope so that by the early 1990s it was providing extension services and education and its fee-paying membership had risen to over 60% of the herders in the country (Umali et al., 1992; Umali and Schwartz, 1994).

Another well-known example in the Anand Milk Union Ltd. (AMUL) in Gujarat, India. This is a milk marketing cooperative initially formed in 1946 by a group of dairy producers aiming to increase the prices they received for their goods. It consists of a three tier cooperative structure owned and managed by member farmers. Village-level Dairy Cooperative Societies (DCS) purchase milk and provide veterinary health services together with artificial insemination and extension advice. District Milk Producers' Unions collect and market milk, provide support to DCSs and are members of an overall Federation. The donor-funded Operation Flood Programme in India has attempted, with a good degree of success, to transfer this model to other states (Umali et al., 1992).

6.2 Economic analysis

There is extensive discussion in almost all the literature about the economic nature of the various veterinary goods (Umali at al, 1992; Leonard, 1985 and 1993; Gros, 1994; James and Upton, 1995). First, the different types of goods need to be identified.

Umali et al. (1992) distinguish between curative health services, preventative health services (subdivided into immunisation, vector control and disease control methods), the provision of veterinary pharmaceuticals and production services (research and extension for improved methods, including artificial insemination). Leonard (1985) refers to this last category as 'promotive services'. Much of the discussion in this area is similar to that in the research and extension sections of this paper. It will not, therefore, be explicitly addressed here.

The two types of goods which are closest to being pure private goods are curative health services and the provision of veterinary pharmaceuticals (which often go hand in hand). In receiving treatment for his/her sick animal an owner reduces the stock of curative services available to others (subtractability) and, at least at first sight, is the sole beneficiary of the services (excludability). However, there are positive externalities, especially in the case of infectious diseases (Gros, 1994). Umali et al. (1992) further disaggregate curative services into diagnosis and treatment. Diagnosis, they argue, involves externalities because by making a diagnosis and communicating it to the animal owner, the veterinarian is increasing the overall level of knowledge in the community – especially important if the illness in question might grow to epidemic proportions (Gros, 1994). Treatment only involves externalities where the illness in question is infectious and can be cured, thereby reducing the risk to other livestock owners. Despite these externalities, however, Umali et al. (1992) do not believe that public provision of curative services is justified.

Gros (1994) concurs with this but gives more emphasis to the private nature of curative services. This, he argues, derives from two factors. First, nobody but the owner of the animal receives immediate economic benefit from the treatment. Second, most of the curative treatment in Africa, in particular, does not involve infectious diseases.

Preventative health services are also largely classified as private goods by Umali et al. (1992), though with the exception of actual vaccine production, they involve externalities. They therefore believe that the extent of public sector intervention should depend upon the type of externality involved and the degree to which the private sector can internalise it (through, for example, membership organisations). Pure public provision is only justified under 'special economic circumstances' such as for zoonotic diseases, foot and mouth disease which might affect exports and tsetse control in open range lands. Otherwise the public sector should back up the primary efforts of the private sector through, for example, subsidising private provision or monitoring compliance. Umali et al. (1992) recognise, however, that because both clinical and preventative services are frequently provided by the same individuals, any subsidy to preventative services might unavoidably spill over to clinical services. Unlike Leonard who sees this as a positive effect (see below), they express concern that it might be used to usher in subsidies to the clinical sector by the back door.

Gros (1994), on the other hand, treats the entire spectrum of preventative care delivery as a public good. His belief is based on the fact that the benefits of action accrue to all meat consumers and livestock producers, this is most obviously for vaccinations but also holds weight for meat inspection and vector control. Preventative care services should therefore be provided by some sort of collectivity in which everyone pays dues, rather than by private bodies.

Leonard (1985) concurs with Gros (1994). He believes that in order to achieve the economically optimum coverage of preventative services their provision should be financed out of taxation. Otherwise, since each individual has an incentive not to inoculate (because of the slight risk of doing so) all individuals will attempt to freeride and the percentage of the population which is inoculated will be sub-optimal (Leonard, 1993). Another issue which Leonard raises is the high discount rates of many African farmers. Their preference for cash in hand today, rather than benefits in the future, is considered by Leonard (1993) to 'violate the rationality assumptions of economic action'. This can only be corrected for by the actions of veterinarians (and by implication the public sector in general) who have more rational (i.e. lower) discount rates and thus a greater appreciation of the value of preventative medicine. Finally, he argues that public sector provision of preventative services has a further benefit in that it increases the scope for private provision of curative services. This is due to the fact that increasing the general level of animal health in a community will increase livestock owners' readiness to pay for individual curative services.

Upton and James (1995) equivocate; they believe that preventative medicine lies somewhere along the public good/private good continuum but lean towards Leonard and Gros's view that external benefits may well be greater than private benefits, especially when the diseases in question are communicable to humans. For this reason they moot the option of imposing a tax on meat consumers to finance services, but reject it on the grounds that it would be too difficult to administer and would reduce the overall demand for meat and thus damage the livestock industry as a whole. They also point out that because of high transport costs to remote areas, the marginal cost of service provision is far lower when programmes are comprehensive than when they are offered on demand in a private capacity. In other words, there exist economies of scale which militate towards public or at least group provision.

Gros (1994) emphasises the fact that the extent to which any particular service can be privatised depends not only upon its 'intrinsic' economic nature, but also the environment in which it exists. This is similar to the argument made about extension services and the stage of development of the country in question. Other factors which Gros argues will be important are: the nature of the prevailing livestock system, herd size, the value of the average animal to its owner, producer concentration in a given area and (this he stresses from his own experience in Cameroun) the receptiveness of high level policy-makers at the livestock ministry.

Gros has collected data from Cameroun which shows that smaller farmers are more likely than larger farmers to be deterred from using a service for which they have to pay. This is not because they value their animals any less (indeed he suggest that they may value them more as a single animal might be the only source of wealth for a small farmer), but simply because they are less able to pay, especially since the costs of servicing them in remote areas are likely to be higher. Umali et al. (1992) add that smaller farmers are more likely to own traditional, rather than modern varieties which are, in general, less susceptible to diseases. In addition, the threat to themselves from contagious disease is lower because of their more extensive production systems and their lower number of animals.

Such reduced demand might imply that economically efficient levels of service provision will not be achieved, if services are entirely privatised. It also has the knock-on effect of reducing the feasibility of establishing and sustaining private veterinary practices in areas where small farmers dominate, which, in turn, further reduces the provision of services. The paper by Odeyemi (1994) looks at the various different types of information which will be necessary to predict whether different areas can sustain a private practice.

Leonard (1993) thus believes that private practice in Africa will only be feasible if organisational arrangements designed to overcome these types of structural constraints are put in place. He believes that costs to individuals must be reduced. This can be done through the use of paraprofessionals and the establishment of veterinary routes to reduce transport costs, but direct government support to private practitioners is also likely to be necessary. It is for this reason that Gros (1994) suggests that the attitude of ministry officials to privatisation is so critical; if they are not in favour of reforms, they can block this support and thus sabotage progress.

Leonard believes that the public sector should sub-contract certain services (e.g. vaccinations) from private practitioners, thereby covering most of the fixed costs they incur and enabling them to offer additional services on a private basis at a lower price. The practitioners might even remain in the public sector, as long as their main contracts are well-specified and include permission to charge for additional services. This would have the added benefit of increasing the motivation of public sector personnel. Leonard recognises that veterinarians might have an incentive to cut down on their publicly financed work in favour of their private work but argues that this is not inevitable. Whether or not it will occur depends on the actual demand for private services and the professional attitude of practitioners (Leonard, 1993).

Leonard also addresses concerns about the fact that in awarding public contracts, governments are effectively granting a cost advantage to a single producer. This might inhibit competition and result in the emergence of geographic monopolists charging extortionate prices. He believes, however, that such problems can be reduced if contracts are bid for at relatively short intervals (he suggests two to five years) and so long as most of the costs of establishing a practice in a certain area can be recouped (so that the incumbent does not have an unfair advantage). He makes a case that most veterinary assets can be transferred or on-sold but this is not convincing when he discusses human capital and client relations in a specific area. He also notes that such a system will fail in the presence of corrupt officials who award contracts according to the bribes they receive (Leonard, 1993).

Finally, there is moral hazard in the market for veterinary services, especially in the areas of drug provision and hygiene inspection, but also in monitoring the quality of the veterinarians themselves. The government, Umali et al. (1992) argue, will be required to provide such services itself, for the benefit of the population at large. Leonard (1993) notes that groups of professionals can regulate themselves, through their associations. Their higher levels of education put them in a better position to do this than many other groups. This will, however, only be feasible where there is adequate competition in the provision of services and where associations are dominated by their better members. Otherwise, one can assume, government regulation will be superior.

6.3 Progress towards new goals
Leonard (1993) believes that it is generally accepted that a veterinary service in Africa will be ineffective if staff salaries represent more than 60% of its budget. If this is true, then countries such as the Central African Republic, where by 1986 staff salaries

accounted for 99.5% of the National Agency for Livestock Development budget, must have had an almost entirely ineffectual service pre-reform (Umali et al., 1992). It is, however, hard to draw general conclusions about the effects of change in the veterinary sector because few country experiences have been documented in any detail, despite the concerted moves towards privatisation throughout the world which are noted by Umali et al. (1992) and Holden et al. (1996).

Those experiences which have been documented are certainly not without fault. In Kenya prior to reform, veterinary services were nominally provided free of charge, but practitioners often withheld provision unless payments were made. When charging was introduced as an official policy the cost to farmers did not necessarily rise but the number of visits made by veterinarians did, implying an increase in productivity on the part of the providers (Leonard, 1985). Other reforms may not have been so beneficial. Kenyan community groups have shown themselves to be good at financing the construction of dips (required to protect cattle against ticks), but not at operating them. In 1983 a survey showed that in areas where dips were operated by local groups 90% of diseases reported were tick related while in areas with government operated dips only 20% of diseases were attributed to ticks. Leonard believes that local herders did not have the technical knowledge required to supervise dips themselves. Leonard also notes problems which occurred in Kenya when cost recovery schemes were established. Neither did veterinary department officials have experience at dealing with money collection, nor were adequate accounting practices established. In addition, public sector veterinarians themselves often failed to make charges for preventative vaccinations as they were more interested in increasing coverage than recovering costs.

In Cameroun, Gros (1994) believes that privatisation and cost recovery programmes were introduced purely to relieve financial pressure on the state, under the influence of donors (the World Bank and the EC in this case) and without regard for improvements in the service provided. Neither veterinarians themselves, nor farmers, were consulted about these major structural changes in provision. Of those livestock ministry policy-makers who were consulted, only 38% wholeheartedly supported the reforms, 52% were neutral (though Gros suggests this was a hedging mechanism by those who opposed the changes but were unable to speak up) and 10% were against. Even at the planning stage little regard was given to accountability. His argument, that reducing the public sector payroll was the key objective, is supported by the fact that instead of starting in the obvious place with a strong push towards privatisation of drug delivery, reforms commenced with a wholesale attack on veterinary service provision. He believes this was because the EC was ready to continue funding drug import and distribution in the public domain, and thus that this was not a drain on state resources. Any gains that might have been made in this area were therefore neglected.

A final problem, experienced by FNEC in the Central African Republic but probably common to other farmers' organisations, is that initial success sometimes leads organisations to expand their activities so much that they become unmanageable. FNEC has suffered from a lack of adequate organisation at the field level, increasing financial pressure and a dearth of members with sufficient education effectively to manage the organisation (Umali et al., 1992).

Nevertheless, the genuine gains in accountability derived from the fact that customers now pay for services – where those services are available – should be noted.

6.4 Focus on the rural poor

Leonard's concerns about whether privatised services will reach the poor appear to be well grounded in countries such as Brazil and Argentina where private supply has proved to be biased towards large and medium scale farmers. The issue of the extent to which user fees deter poorer farmers from drawing on services is, however, less clear cut. Umali et al. (1992) cite contrary evidence from Kenya (two studies of dipping are mentioned, in only one did fees reduce demand) and a World Bank study of rinderpest vaccination in ten African countries which shows there to be no significant depressing effect on demand from cost recovery.

Where NGO efforts have supplemented public and private services, the poor, who formerly had no access to services, have benefited. In Bangladesh, the NGO Proshika works with groups providing training in cattle rearing and disease control, vaccinations (with some cost recovery) and livestock insurance (although this is not proving popular). In addition they have set up research farms. By 1991 they claimed to have benefited over 12,000 households (Khan et al., 1991).

Intermediate Technology's programmes in both India and Kenya are based upon the belief that many bovine diseases are treatable by trained farmers. They have therefore operated training programmes and opened shops which sell veterinary drugs to expand the poorer people's access to at least some form of veterinary advice (Grandin et al., 1991). Such deregulation has been one of the most beneficial aspects of change as far as poorer people are concerned. Paraveterinarians usually operate at lower cost and also, because they represent new competition, may force fully qualified veterinarians to lower their prices. Perhaps the greatest impediment to such change is the attitude of veterinarians themselves – losing their monopoly may be threatening for them, although it is more common for them to justify their resistance to change in terms of threats to animal health rather than to their own private interest and status. The same problem has been faced by those working in family planning where doctors have been reluctant to allow people with lesser qualifications to provide advice.

What is notable, though, is that much of the attention in the veterinary sector is devoted to larger animals, in particular cattle. Poorer people may own cattle but a greater proportion of them probably own goats and chickens. To the extent that problems relating to these animals are ignored, poorer people fail to benefit from change. In addition, the focus within the livestock area on veterinary services to the (relative) exclusion of livestock extension and the development of livestock marketing options also reduces the benefits to poor people from the changes. There is, though, an increasing recognition of the need for change which may improve the prospects of poorer people over the longer term.

6.5 Lessons

Once more the key lesson that can be drawn from experiences thus far is that there are no widely applicable blueprints for reform and each country will have different requirements. For example the World Bank tried to transfer the successful model of the India's Anand Milk Union Ltd. to Pakistan in the late 1970s. Project performance was held to be 'very inadequate' (Umali et al., 1992), partly because of political rivalries amongst the agencies involved and partly because of inadequate commitment on behalf of the Punjab government. A first step in any process of reform is likely to be to conduct an assessment of what animal health services are already available in any given community (including traditional healers etc.) and what the vested interests of the different regulatory and supervisory bodies area.

This last issue was important in determining the outcome of reform in Cameroun (Gros, 1994). There, Ministry officials had little faith in the programme and even less expertise with which to support it. Since there were no existing private veterinarians in the country there were no models to follow and those who were supposed to administer reform were veterinarians rather than economists or accountants. Thus, after four years only twelve of the country's 112 veterinarians had set up private practice and producer cooperatives had not emerged to take on any of the former public sector functions. Those veterinarians who did move to the private sector had no government support – at best they were advised by international pharmaceutical companies. Finally, the banking system in the country was crippled at the time and thus potential private providers could not secure credit for their new enterprises.

It is clearly important that adequate attention is paid to supporting the process of reform and to building political will behind efforts to privatise. The time taken to do this should not be underestimated. It will also be important to ensure that existing and new vets have access to training on business/marketing skills, something that they are quite unlikely to have learned during traditional veterinary training. Veterinary curricula may need to be adjusted so that those qualifying gain a wide range of preventative and production-oriented skills to sell to prospective clients. Even when trainees are equipped with such skills it may be appropriate to provide them with particular incentives to work in remote areas, as suggested above. Certainly it will be important for the public services to operate a consistent policy on private practice. It is almost never attractive to establish private practice in an area where there is subsidised or free public provision, or the danger of this being reinstated at any moment.

One issue that has received a good deal of attention is that of the relationship between paraveterinarians, where these exist, and fully-trained veterinarians. It is important, first, that customers can distinguish between the different types of providers so that they know what service they can expect. It is also important that links should be maintained between paravets and full vets so that technical backup is available when required. A focus for discussion has been on the extent to which paravets should be permitted to sell veterinary drugs: many veterinarians argue that they should be prevented from selling any drugs at all. Although the arguments may be couched in terms of animal health they also have a good deal to do with the profit associated with selling drugs. If it is these profits which enable private veterinarians to operate there may be good reason for maintaining them. However, it is clearly logical that paravets have access to a limited class of drugs, both to improve their effectiveness of service and also to help them maintain their own income streams.

Finally, the role of veterinary professional associations has also received quite some attention in discussions of reform. Such associations clearly have a role to play in regulation and quality control. They have existed in many countries for a long time but they must now adapt to accommodate the needs of dispersed private practitioners. Whether or not they accept paravets as full or partial members remains a moot point (FAO Email conference on Principles for Rational Delivery of Public and Private Veterinary Services, 1997).

7. Rural credit

7.1 Changes in supply or supplier

The supply of rural credit is usually divided into 'formal' and 'informal' sectors. The former, which is the main focus of this review, includes banks, government agencies, cooperative credit unions, NGOs and, frequently in the past, monopsonistic marketing parastatals which would provide credit and deduct repayments at source from the following year's crop sales. The informal sector is made up largely of individuals (traders, landlords or farmers themselves) who lend money as a business. They are traditionally characterised as being highly usurious and in positions of considerable power due to lack of local competition, although some would dispute that (Yaron, 1992a; Poulton et al., 1997).

In the credit area recent changes have been due both to the reform of marketing parastatals and increased criticism of public sector credit programmes characterised by very high costs and poor recovery rates. In losing their monopsonistic position, parastatals have lost their presumed competitive advantage in credit supply (if principal and interest recovery are delinked from output sales the risk to parastatals is as high as to any other body providing credit) and governments facing huge bills for subsidising credit programmes in turbulent economic times have withdrawn. For example, the Government of Brazil was, at times, spending more than one quarter of its entire agricultural budget to maintain the rural credit system (Yaron, 1992a). Cleaver (1993) reports that most World Bank agricultural credit programmes in Africa have failed.

What is less clear is the extent to which the gap left by the withdrawal of government has been filled in different areas and if it has been filled, whether this is by the formal or informal sector. World Bank projects are still working through public institutions (Cleaver, 1993), but projects are now part of overall financial reform programmes, institution building and rural savings mobilisation. Yaron (1992a) reports successful credit schemes in Indonesia and Thailand where over a very short period of time it has been possible to finance lending largely out of voluntary rural savings. To this extent the source of supply of credit within the formal sector has changed. In many places the actual supply of money is self-financing (ie. within an integrated savings an credit organisation there is no need for external capital to be raised), although continued subsidies to cover operating costs are required in most places (despite the great emphasis on achieving overall sustainability).

These types of schemes supplement the many existing rotating savings and credit associations (ROSCAs), savings and credit cooperatives (SACCOs) and other similarly structured organisations which exist in rural areas in developing countries. The main variations between these types of organisation lie in whether or not they provide voluntary savings facilities (as opposed to savings being deposited only to be drawn out as a loan when the depositor's 'turn' comes around) and in the ownership structures of the organisation. Traditionally cooperatives have functioned on the 'one member, one vote' principle, though a new model of Financial Services Associations is emerging in which members' votes are proportional to the share capital they own (Rogaly, 1997). Financial Services Associations and organisations which offer voluntary savings facilities will tend to endure (so long as they remain viable) while some rotating schemes operate only for a fixed period of time (until everyone has drawn a loan). In a sense, then, these organisations straddle the formal and informal sectors.

Donors and both north- and south-based NGOs are also funding cooperative credit institutions which rely on savings mobilisation. Some, such as Benin's Rural Savings and Loan or BRAC's schemes in Bangladesh, are outside the public sector entirely while others, such as Ghana's Rural Banks, have minority government participation. Cleaver (1993) reports that the World Bank has begun directly to support private sector credit activities. In some cases it subsidises not the loans themselves but helps to cover the transaction costs incurred by lenders and borrowers. The idea is that although new savings and loans institutions might need some support at the outset, especially in the provision of central liquidity funds, staff training and the establishment of viable accounting practices, actual lending operations should not be subsidised. The danger of subsidising loans as part of an initial support package is that institutions become accustomed to making lending decisions which are not strictly economic. This threatens their long-run security and sustainability (Yaron, 1992b). While transactions costs are subsidised by external organisations, efforts are also underway to reduce these, while at the same time increasing repayment rates.

7.2 Economic analysis

Credit may be a private good in the sense that it is excludable and subtractable, but these attributes are not necessarily sufficient to make it attractive to private suppliers. This is because the credit market combines the problems of imperfect information and risk (Smith and Thomson, 1991). In developing countries this risk derives especially from the poor legal frameworks for loan recovery and securing collateral (Yaron, 1992a). Risk aversion in the private sector leads to the provision of credit only to those with better access to collateral or particular ties to the lenders. It also leads to high borrowing costs which reduce the demand for credit.

In principle the government should be less risk-averse than the private sector because it covers a wider geographical area (agricultural failure due to climate or pest outbreaks tends to be geographically concentrated) and has a longer time horizon. Smith and Thomson (1991) would also argue that it has greater powers of coercion and therefore a better chance of securing repayment. It should, therefore, be a more efficient lender. However, it is generally disadvantaged in comparison to the private sector in terms of detailed knowledge of local conditions and lack of any sense of loyalty on the part of borrowers (Smith and Thomson, 1991). This reduces its ability to guard against adverse selection where those who are most likely to default are the most eager to seek credit.[3] This problem raises the overall cost of borrowing for others and further increases the likelihood that lenders will require borrowers to put up collateral (Yaron, 1992a).

Yaron (1992a) suggests that governments have used the arguments about their own ability to bear risk to justify the provision of subsidised rural credit. They have aimed to increase equity (particularly to compensate for the 'urban bias' of other policies) through credit programmes, and in so doing sponsor growth which would otherwise be constrained by lack of capital investment by farmers. It is this assumption – that rural economies are credit constrained – which Yaron particularly disputes. He believes that since most new technologies are divisible, credit constraints are not severe. On the contrary, he argues that the success of schemes such as those in Indonesia and Thailand demonstrate that it is functioning rural savings institutions which are really lacking. Furthermore he argues that informal lenders do face significant competition and are, in general, not as exploitative as they are usually portrayed to be.

He also points out that because subsidised loans often end up in the hands of the relatively richer people with broader economic interests, they have proved to be an extremely inefficient way of raising investment in agriculture. Two World Bank OED studies found that of the Bank funds provided through credit projects in Mexico, Pakistan and the Philippines only 25–50% were estimated to have added to agricultural investment (Yaron, 1992b).

Thus, rather than providing credit itself at subsidised rates, and thereby reducing the opportunities for the development of a functioning private credit system, the public sector should focus on reducing the risk that individual lenders face. This it should do through improving physical infrastructure (improving transport and information systems to facilitate inter-regional trade should reduce commodity price fluctuation), improving enforcement mechanisms for loan collection and focusing on commodity risk mitigating arrangements. The public sector may also need to provide some transitional support for institutions during the process of reform of the financial system, although Yaron (1992a) explicitly cautions against long-term provision of funds.

Another risk-reducing mechanism is the small group. Many of the success stories in rural credit provision, such as systems in Korea and Taiwan and the Grameen and BRAC schemes in Bangladesh, have relied on such groups. The main advantages of groups are that members share detailed knowledge of each others circumstances and a social cohesiveness which, especially if coupled with collective responsibility for all loans, reduce the risk of default (especially when the source of loans is members' own savings). It is also possible to establish elaborate ritual within such groups which can

---

[3] In this incidence of adverse selection lenders take the role of purchasers – with incomplete information – and borrowers the role of vendors.

itself contribute to improving repayment rates (Jain, 1992). A further advantage is the transparency of relationships between lenders and borrowers within the group environment (Johnson and Rogaly, 1997). Yaron (1992a) suggests channelling World Bank spending for credit institutions through such organisations. It should be noted, however, that there are plenty of credit schemes which have been modelled after the Grameen scheme which have failed; the suitability of groups is a function of underlying social relations and the distances that must be covered to participate in group activities, amongst other things (Hulme and Mosely, 1996). Group cohesiveness must be genuine if benefits are to be forthcoming. Externally inspired cooperative credit schemes have usually failed in the same way as other public sector efforts to provide credit.

7.3 Progress towards new goals

The new types of credit institution which have taken over where the public sector has withdrawn or where it never penetrated, do seem to be more efficient. While old public sector agencies were judged in terms of loan disbursement, new commercial lenders must meet profit objectives. The staff at Indonesia's successful Bank Rakyat Indonesia – Unit Desa are rewarded in part according to branch financial performance.

Existing public sector systems such as the Thai Bank for Agriculture and Agriculture Cooperatives have also become more efficient by reforming their financial reporting and administrative systems. While over 50% of the loans made through the cooperative system in Thailand were in arrears in the 1980s, the Bank now has a 'high loan recovery rate' and its running costs are equal to only 4% of its total assets. This contrasts with public sector lending in Mexico where transaction costs at one stage exceeded the amount of money loaned (Yaron, 1992a).

The extent of financial sustainability of new types of financial service providers should not, however, be overstated. For all the Grameen bank's success it is far from being self-sustaining. Indeed Johnson and Rogaly (1997) are cautious in their emphasis on financial sustainability because the believe that, if too zealously pursued, this goal might reduce the prospects for financial service provision in poorer areas. While viable commercial interest rates probably should be charged, there may be a continuing need for external support to cover running costs.

Institutions which are able to mobilise rural savings do so because they provide attractive interest rates and security as well as ease of access (because of their relative proximity to depositors). In the past rural people have often had no opportunities for savings and have thus been forced into inefficient uses of their money, for example saving with no interest at home (and thus losing out where inflation is high) or, frequently, investing in livestock. Although there are cultural and also economic reasons (it can be very profitable) why people invest in livestock this strategy can also be very risky. This is especially the case where general animal health is not good and the increase in livestock populations which it implies leads to over-grazing and crop damage.

Generally, then the move away from credit provision, *per se*, to providing a wider range of financial services – including savings facilities – should have a positive impact upon overall effectiveness in meeting rural people's needs. Bringing together saving and lending also enables institutions to develop relationships with their clients before they take on any lending risk. They thereby incur loyalty and gain critical information about potential borrowers. Savers themselves learn about how financial institutions function and become accustomed to the discipline of making regular payments. This contributes to overall system efficiency as does the reduced emphasis on monitoring the purposes to which loans are put.

Within financial services organisations, the importance of training staff so that they understand the basic principles which underlie their work has been recognised. This means that staff operate more effectively. It also enables managers to delegate greater authority to field level staff to make lending decisions and to adapt schemes to take into account local needs and circumstances (still adhering to the core principles of lending at market rates and seeking to make financial service organisations sustainable over the longer term) (Padmanabhan, 1988).

When it comes to accountability, many of the newer types of financial service organisation are clearly way ahead of old style centralised projects of national banking systems. Financial services are increasingly being brought to the rural areas enabling borrowers and savers to develop direct relationships with local level staff. These staff are themselves empowered to make decisions on day-to-day matters, decisions which reflect local needs. Even more important, though, is the fact that many of the newer types of financial service organisations are directly owned and operated by member-shareholders.

7.4 Focus on the rural poor

Even when credit was subsidised, it was usually not the poorest who benefited, whatever the stated intentions of governments (Yaron, 1992a). Artificially low, sometimes negative, interest rates and little pressure to repay meant that the demand for credit often exceeded supply (Yaron, 1992a). In such situations it was often the more influential farmers whose demands were met first. Furthermore, the transaction costs associated with accessing formal loans may be so high that informal loans end up being cheaper, however high the nominal interest rates. A study in Bangladesh has shown that the average effective cost of a loan smaller than 1,000 takas varied between 146% and 169% in the formal market, while it varied between 57% to 86% in the informal market (study by Z. Ahmed cited in Yaron 1992b). Indeed some formal lenders do not even countenance such small loans, whether or not farmers are willing to bear their share of the transaction costs.

Therefore increased institutional support to groups and local associations which rely on members' savings to finance loans should benefit the rural poor by improving their access to credit and lowering the costs of borrowing. Such systems rely on group dynamics to ensure loan repayment. This reduces the need for collateral and therefore gives access to credit to landless labourers and women whose land may be in their husbands' names. For example the Grameen Bank loans exclusively to landless individuals, 90% of whom are women. Loan recovery rates are in the region of 98%.

The move to consider not just credit, as a stand alone intervention, but the provision of an integrated rural financial services network is potentially very important to the poor. Often poor people require small amounts of money to tide them over during difficult times and it is important that they should have a financial network upon which they can rely to provide this. In the past the aim of credit schemes was to increase the productive potential of beneficiaries and so to stimulate economic growth in rural areas. Increasingly, though, there is a recognition of the risk-reducing benefits of financial service provision (Hulme and Mosely, 1996). Less attention is being paid to monitoring the exact uses to which loans are put. This saves valuable resources and reflects a recognition that the important issue is whether a borrower can afford to pay back a loan, not how the money is used. Loans are frequently repaid out of regular income rather than out of the productive use of the invested loan itself (Johnson and Rogaly, 1997).

Nevertheless, Hulme and Mosely (1996) argue that existing credit schemes do not adequately reach the poorest. They feel that some progress in this direction has been made but that we require further innovation if greater success is to be achieved. Existing credit schemes, which they argue are becoming too homogenous around the Grameen model, do not adequately differentiate between borrowers to enable them to target the very poorest. Nor do they include sufficient risk-reducing mechanisms to enable the very poorest to benefit. It remains true that there are few successful credit schemes operating in rural areas of Africa. It is in these areas that climate induced risks tend to be at their highest and opportunities for earning income off farm at their lowest. It is here also that many of the poorest live. Rogaly (1997) also concurs with the view that the poorest do not always gain adequately from the provision of rural financial services. He does, though, stress that some of the newer models of village banks seem to be increasing their outreach amongst poorer groups. In the final analysis, however, the very poorest may never have adequate debt-bearing capacity to take on loans and it would be damaging to insist that they should do so.

7.5 Lessons

There is no universal formula for the provision of financial services to poorer people, though there is an increasing consensus that: as far as possible interest rates should be market determined; lending agencies should be decentralised; externally-sponsored schemes should take account of and build on existing informal methods of accessing credit which have proved successful over time and which provide an indication of the debt-bearing capacity of local people; and that credit and savings schemes should be provided in tandem as key components of a broader financial service infrastructure. This will help to ensure that local capital is productively utilised and will assist local people to meet different needs at different times.

Perhaps the clearest lesson that can be drawn in this area is that rural savings *can* provide a viable basis for lending. Indeed, even if mobilisation of rural savings is not cost-effective in the short term, its costs should be borne as part of the investment required to create a viable system; it is, in effect, an investment in human capital (Asian Productivity Organisation, 1992; Egaitsu, 1992; Vogel, 1992). Another lesson is that loans extended for 'non-productive uses' (e.g. funerals, weddings and to cover hungry periods in the agricultural calendar) are not necessarily more insecure than loans with a more obvious income-generating focus. In Mali 75% of the Kafo Jiginiew savings and loan organisation's loans are extended on a short-term basis to cover the hungry period between cotton planting and receipt of cotton revenues. The repayment rate is consistently over 99% (Kafo Jiginiew, 1994).

An important consideration in establishing a sustainable rural financial network is that borrowers should believe in the long-term commitment of the lending institution. If they do so, they are far less likely to default. It is also important that the provision of credit is not tied up with other political motives and that providing organisations do not have unfavourable reputations based on their previous activities elsewhere. One complicating factor for NGOs can be that credit provision is just one among a number of socially-oriented interventions; it can be hard for NGOs to exact payment from those with whom they are working, and on whom they may rely, in other areas of activity.

Finally, it should be pointed out that many credit institutions, both new and old style, continue to fail. It is also worth re-emphasising the fact that many of the more successful providers of financial services do not, or have not yet, reached the poorest. For both these reasons it is imperative that continued efforts are made to design more effective institutions, better matched to their local environments, and better able to serve those clients who face the greatest degree of risk.

8. Agricultural produce marketing

8.1 Changes in supply or supplier

The focus of change in marketing systems has been the abolition or reform of monopsonistic parastatals, particularly in Africa. The degree of success in dismantling these has varied in different countries and for different crops. In Tanzania, for example, the National Milling Corporation's share of marketed maize dropped from 90% to 2% in a relatively short time (Mans, 1994), though of the export crops only cashew marketing had been liberalised by the early 1990s. In Kenya the progress in maize reform has been less smooth. The National Cereals and Produce Board was reformed in the 1980s, but in 1992 movement controls on maize were reimposed and maize was reoffered to millers at subsidised prices, undercutting the nascent private sector (Swamy, 1994).

In most countries, even during the time that private trade was outlawed, traders existed. Parallel market prices for controlled crops were frequently high, because of shortages. This allowed traders to make supra-normal profits which justified the risks of operation. Now that markets have been liberalised new entrants have begun trading (Smith and Thomson, 1991). Not all, however, are individual commercial operators. Especially in Latin America, commodity organisations and cooperatives such as Bolivia's El Ceibo, (the federation of cocoa producing cooperatives) provide marketing and processing services to their members.

In various African countries smaller self-help organisations (farmer controlled enterprises) have entered the commercial area, some with external assistance and others on their own. Their levels of success have varied considerably with factors such as internal group dynamics and existing skills and experience of group members being critical. Also important is groups' relationships with the private sector more broadly and their ability to access working capital. Stringfellow et al. (1997) found that a strong business orientation was important to the success of groups as was a degree of autonomy from donors.

Although there has been a keen response from private traders in many areas and for many commodities, the extent to which marketing problems continue to plague producers in developing countries (particularly in sub-Saharan Africa) should not be under-estimated. In more remote areas with poor infrastructure few traders have established themselves and those which have tend to pay low prices to farmers who have few other options. Unfortunately it is in just these areas that groups of farmers are least likely to demonstrate the positive characteristics mentioned in the previous paragraph. Poulton et al. are, however, reasonably optimistic about private trade in the major cash crops in the future. They suggest that traders have been far quicker to respond to output marketing opportunities than they have been to openings in input supply, they do point out, though, the importance of working capital and the fact that where this is available to traders progress towards competitive markets is much faster than elsewhere. As a result it is often businessmen with overseas connections who are the first entrants. This is true both of the Tanzanian cashew market (where all domestic traders are Asian-Tanzanians) and the Ghanaian cocoa market.

8.2 Economic analysis

Buying and selling physical goods is at the very heart of private sector activities. However, the agricultural sector has some special characteristics which can be argued to militate towards public sector intervention (Smith and Thomson, 1991).

First, it is inherently risky and because of high covariance of risk in any geographical area and issues of seasonality, prices can fluctuate enormously (Thomson, 1991; Smith and Thomson, 1991). Governments often justify their intervention on the grounds of price (and hence income) stabilisation. Second, agricultural policies partly determine national food supplies. Many governments feel that they are too critical to be left to the vagaries of the market and intervene to secure buffer stocks, frequently operated and administered through marketing parastatals (Thomson, 1991). Third, production is extremely dispersed. Governments often justify intervention to protect small farmers, who are more likely than others to suffer from a lack of information and from exploitation by traders (Smith and Thomson, 1991). Finally, agriculture dominates many developing countries. Governments, can therefore argue that efforts to increase equity should be focused in this sector (i.e. that social policy should be effected through the agricultural sector). Thus they rationalise the operation of pan-territorial pricing and purchasing policies.

Many of these problems could, however, be partially addressed without direct intervention by the public sector. Governments could focus on increasing the flow of information (e.g. with marketing bulletins on public radio) and improving rural infrastructure to make far-flung communities more accessible. They could promote risk-reducing technologies, such as irrigation, and improve the legal foundation and enforceability of contract systems. They could also make agricultural trade more attractive to private commercial companies, through deregulation of import and export, including removing currency controls, and reducing domestic bureaucratic procedures. This would, in turn, reduce the likelihood of exploitative geographical monopolies and cartels developing. It would also indirectly enhance the likelihood that such companies would invest in research and provide extension as a way to gain advantage over the competition.

However, in the interests of general social welfare, complete government withdrawal may not be advisable. It is often critical for the public sector to maintain some influence on the supply of basic foods, particularly to ensure that poorer and more remote areas are serviced by marketing systems (both for supply and purchasing). While in Asia, where population density tends to be much greater, private trade may be sufficiently well-developed to cater to most areas, however small the local market, this is usually not the case in Africa. As marketing parastatals have renounced their monopolies in places such as Tanzania, distant villages have remained almost untouched by private trade (Mans, 1994). In Latin America large farmers' associations and cooperatives have developed an important role in marketing of cash crops (for example El Ceibo in Bolivia). Although there are some viable self-help organisations in Africa, they are generally more underdeveloped in this continent. They also tend to have less influence where food crops are concerned.

Even in countries where irrigation is extremely common and basic food crops are harvested two or three times during the year, seasonal price fluctuations are still significant. This is the case for rice in Indonesia where, despite a well developed private market, traders have been reluctant to exploit the opportunities for inter-seasonal price arbitrage. Indeed it has been argued that very limited intervention by the parastatal BULOG to stabilise prices has reduced the risk, rather than the trading opportunities, of private individuals and companies and hence had a positive influence on their involvement (Ellis, 1993).

8.3 Progress towards new goals

In those areas where marketing responsibility has been withdrawn from monopolistic parastatals, increases in efficiency (largely as a result of reductions in rent-seeking) do seem to be apparent. In particular, consumers (including many small farmers) have benefited from overall increases in trade and supply of staples and therefore more stable food prices (Quiroz and Valdes, 1995). Nevertheless, there can still be significant fluctuation and therefore genuine efficiency benefits to be gained from continued (though modified) intervention in food crop marketing.

Timmer (1992) argues that while there are no good arguments for keeping food prices either substantially above or below their long-run opportunity costs in world markets, 'policies that stabilize food prices along the long-run trend in world market prices have the potential to contribute simultaneously to both economic efficiency (and growth) and improved income distribution through better nutritional welfare of the poor'. He emphasises the non-market benefits to poor people of *stable* food prices, arguing that when food costs represent a large component of any individual's or household's budget, any change in prices will necessitate a substantial reallocation of resources. The transactions costs of effecting such a reallocation will be high and should be included as a negative component of the consumer's welfare function. In addition, Timmer (1992) maintains that if consumers are confident of food price stability they will be less likely to invest in low productivity, highly liquid, ''precautionary savings' such as jewellery, gold and, in rural areas, livestock.

The fact that not all areas are attractive to new entrants also reduces the efficiency gains from reform. In Mali, Smith and Thomson (1991) observe that traders have been deterred from entering markets because of demand and supply instability, regulatory uncertainty and the unenforceability of contracts. In both Tanzania and Mali traders are reported to be risk-averse and unwilling (or unable because of their lack of access to capital) to invest in storage. This results in increased risk to farmers who are forced to store more of their produce on farm. The worst scenario for farmers is that they are forced to store beyond the period when their goods remain viable because the parastatal has withdrawn and no trader has taken its place. Governments must clearly be aware of this possibility and ensure the intervention of the public sector where the private sector does not exist. There should be good scope for transferring or selling off redundant public storage facilities to the private sector. Indeed, where this does not happen it is likely to increase traders' and potential traders' unease about the intentions of the public sector (the chance that the public sector agencies might re-enter the market).

8.4 Focus on the rural poor

The efficiency of agricultural marketing services is important to everyone. There are very few people who neither purchase nor sell agricultural produce (in particular foodstuffs) at some stage in the year or who would not wish there to be an efficient service in place should they need to call upon it. To the extent, then, that market reforms have improved the overall efficiency of services the poor should have benefited as much as anyone.

Much of the pressure for reform came from critics who held that parastatal or public sector marketing systems were directly damaging the interests of rural people – including the rural poor – because they were keeping farmgate prices artificially low to benefit the urban middle classes consumers. For this reason, the rural poor might be assumed to have benefited relatively more than others. However, since most of the rural poor also purchase food at times during the year when their resources are at their lowest, the equation is not quite as simple as it might initially have seemed. Certainly any drop in the price of food which assists people to meet recommended food intake levels will bring them a disproportionate benefit (on the assumption that there is diminishing marginal utility of food consumption and that there is greater utility in meeting one's basic food needs than in other expenditures). Correspondingly, a rise in food prices during the hungry season may have a disproportionately large negative effect upon the poor.

When it comes to cash crops marketing Poulton et al. (1997) note that liberalisation has generally benefited farmers though not the poorest farmers (who are often not able to grow cash crops because of their lack of access to capital to finance input purchase). They argue, in particular, that the 'interlocking' of markets (whereby private purchasers of produce supply inputs on credit to farmers) need not be associated with exploitation of farmers as has frequently been assumed. Key variables in the equation are: the nature and degree of competition between traders; the extent of alternative income-generation opportunities available to farmers; traders' investment in specific assets; the availability of information at the farm-gate; and non-market social relations between traders and farmers. When farmers are well-informed and have other choices and traders are competing to purchase outputs, partly because they have made significant investments in processing or similar, then 'interlocking' markets can benefit farmers just as much as traders.

Because these and many other factors vary, it is not possible to draw any general conclusions about the equity effects of marketing reform or the direction in which prices will go post-reform. Indeed, it has rarely been possible to predict the overall impact of marketing reform. This makes it particularly important that monitoring systems are set up in parallel with any reform efforts. These systems should seek to monitor not just aggregate supply responses but also the effects of reform on particular groups of producers/consumers. If certain groups are observed to suffer unduly they may subsequently require targeted assistance (not necessarily to support agricultural production which may prove uneconomic under the new circumstances, but to secure their livelihoods in some form while they adjust to change, for example if local processing facilities are closed). However, the danger of increased dependence of such groups upon food aid, or similar, should also be borne in mind. Blench (1998) notes that one of the impacts of the Economic Structural Adjustment Programme – together with recent drought – in north east Zimbabwe has been to increase local people's reliance on external assistance even in 'normal' years. As people become used to receiving such assistance they begin to factor it into their livelihood strategies. One result of this can be that structurally dysfunctional households survive rather than seeking other more viable options to sustain themselves.

8.5 Lessons

Although there is no blueprint for state involvement in marketing systems, it seems generally true to say that intervention in cash crops marketing is not advantageous. Poulton et al. (1997) support this view. Indeed they argue that even where it might be desirable that the state retains some long-run role in market regulation, complete withdrawal can be the most beneficial short-term strategy. They believe that this will increase investor confidence and help to eliminate the culture of rent-seeking that pervades in many state organisations (although they also acknowledge that there may be environmental justification for regulation of markets which tips the balance back in favour of continuity in state regulation). They also stress the importance of 'a regular and constructive dialogue between officials and traders'.

The situation for basic food crops is more complex as impacts are far more widely felt. A certain number of lessons may be learned from the Indonesian example. BULOG's success in operationalising floor prices for rice is held to be due to its excellent price monitoring, its relatively quick response time to market conditions and the general reliability of its defence of floor prices. It is also very specific about the location and times of its purchases – it buys only between 3% and 8% of peak season production – and can thus limit the extent of its overhead (although this is still criticised). In this way it simultaneously intervenes in markets while promoting free trade and – most crucially for producers – competition.

Once more, it seems, attention must be focused first on clear definition of ends and only then on selecting the most cost effective way of achieving these. Nonetheless, it must be emphasised that, despite all the work that has gone in this area, no generally applicable formula for marrying buffer stock activity with private sector enterprise has yet been found.

One thing that is clear is that effecting change, particularly in food crop marketing systems, is extremely difficult. These systems impact upon almost everyone within a country and reform is thus likely to be most contentious. Lewa (1995) points out the importance of constructing reform programmes very gradually, paying attention to detail and assuring consistency both internally and between donors' policies. Internal consistency requires an integrated programme of support to would-be traders (for example, ensuring that they can access start-up capital and storage facilities, that they are not over-burdened with regulation and that their support organisations, such as chambers of commerce, are free to operate as they wish). It also entails the establishment of public intervention policies which are predictable and transparent (such as well-publicised floor prices). Donors for their part must ensure that their own exports or food aid provisions do not undermine nascent private markets. Lewa also deems it extremely important to devote attention to building support for reform amongst a country's politicians (and not just the bureaucracy which is what he perceives as having happened in Kenya).

Finally, it should be noted that many of the key issues in agricultural marketing are generic to the economy as a whole. In order for private trade to flourish there must be a viable market infrastructure in place (including definition of weights and measures and contract enforcement mechanisms) and effective transport and information systems (a public information and statistical service to help farmers make rational planting decisions and a road or railway system which will reduce the costs imposed upon traders). There should also be economic and financial stability and a financial system which can supply capital to bona fide borrowers at a reasonable cost. Many developing countries lack all or most of these crucial characteristics and therefore effectively lack the preconditions for a viable and *inclusive* private trading system to develop.

9. Conclusion

This literature survey has looked at the evolving relationship between the state and the individual in the context of the supply of agricultural goods and supporting services. Whilst in the past public sector agencies were frequently the only providers of all manner of goods and services, and individuals were consequently very dependent upon them, there is now far more choice and a philosophy of institutional pluralism prevails.

This review has attempted to cover most of the goods and services which are critical to rural people who depend upon natural resources for their livelihoods; it is clearly not exhaustive. There are many goods which are less easily defined but nonetheless critical to rural people, such as general skill levels for the management of natural resources and environmental goods. This latter category would include the preservation of genetic diversity and soil fertility, both of which are of enormous importance to rural people in the longer term. Furthermore, while stressing the importance of considering the overall livelihoods of rural people (rather than just their natural-resource based activities) this paper itself has not gone into any detail about non-agricultural livelihood options nor has it considered mechanisms or options for service delivery in related areas.

The review covers a sector in which there has been widespread change and draws a number of preliminary lessons from the change process. It also yields two key conclusions. The first is that pursuing increases in efficiency, which provide the dominant rationale for change, may be antithetical to social equity unless specific safeguards are built in and a broad definition of the concept of efficiency itself is adopted. Efficiency is usually sought through the market mechanism and this itself has major failings; it is often the poorest who suffer most. The second conclusion is that while there may be no blueprints for the roles of different actors, there is a growing pool of experience upon which decision-makers can draw. Furthermore, economic theory can help with early identification of areas where continued government involvement is likely to be desirable. Table 4 summarises the economic analysis presented in this paper.

Partly due to the many market failures identified, there are no areas of service provision in which complete government withdrawal appears prudent. At the very least public sector agencies must manage the markets; they are often the only bodies with the scope and the authority to enforce the necessary regulation. They also have a role in facilitating the entry of new players, especially in those countries where private sector trade and the infrastructure which underpins it have been severely undermined over the past decades. Private sectors and farmers' organisations – both of which have formerly been considered subversive elements in many countries – need administrative, institutional and financial assistance to transform them into fully functioning members of the Agricultural Technology System. This 'facilitating' role

Table 4: Summary of sub-sector discussions: economic analysis

	Economic characteristics		Other relevant market failures
	Private	*Non-private*	
Fertiliser			
• Trade	✓		• Risk
			• Capital market imperfections
• Best practices information		✓	• Negative externalities
Seeds			
• Research	✓	✓	• Risk
• Supply	✓	✓	• Capital market imperfections
• Regulation	(✓)	✓	• Moral hazard
			• Adverse selection
Research			
• Pre-technology		✓	• Risk
• Prototype technology	✓	✓	• Economies of scale
• Usable technology	✓	(✓)	
Extension			
• Broadly applicable		✓	• Lumpy purchase
• Highly specific	✓		• Adverse selection
Veterinary Services			
• Curative	✓		• Externalities
• Preventative	(✓)	✓	• Moral hazard
• Promotive	(✓)	(✓)	• Economies of scale
Rural Credit			
• Credit supply	✓		• Risk
			• Adverse selection
Marketing Services			
• Food crops	✓	(✓)	• Risk
• Cash crops	✓		• Imperfect information
			• Capital market imperfections

of the state, and how it is best operationalised, is receiving increasing attention in the late 1990s. Both the World Bank's 1997 World Development Report (entitled *The*

State in a Changing World) and the recent UK White Paper on International Development have moved forward the debate in this area. The White Paper argues that: 'There is now an opportunity to create a new synthesis which builds on the role of the State in facilitating economic growth and benefiting the poor'.

The emphasis is, though, on facilitation. It is only where other suppliers do not exist (possibly because of market failures) or where the narrow economic efficiency implied by dependence on markets is not felt to be socially acceptable that the government itself should become a supplier. The foregoing economic analysis together with a basic understanding of who in a country has purchasing power gives some early indications as to where this might be the case. Public sector agencies must, however, recognise that it will often be in the areas in which they have had least success in the past that they will have the greatest role in the future. The fact that they might wish to withdraw from these does not mean that it will be efficient for them to do so.

In particular the poorest living in the most remote areas will tend to be ill-served by markets. Among these will be many women who, in most countries, have very little access to cash since they are limited to household and food crop activities. Because of the marginal environments in which they live, these people tend to have the most complex needs. The gulf between them and government researchers and extensionists is far wider than for prosperous farmers and accountability is hard to achieve. Indeed it is precisely because these people have been so poorly served by public sector institutions that much of the pressure for reform has come about. Governments will therefore need to identify and find new ways of addressing problems in such areas if their efforts are to be effective.

This conclusion, that the role of the state in developing countries should be to regulate and monitor markets with a view to more direct intervention only in those areas in which the market underprovides is, then, easy to reach but extremely difficult to operationalise. Governments have been unable effectively to monitor, manage and regulate their own efforts in the past. It is not clear how they should be expected to be able to do this for others now, especially since the greater number and type of actors involved is likely to increase the complexity of the system. Leonard (1993) insinuates that the World Bank does not pay adequate attention to issues of regulation under market imperfections. He also notes the enormous volume of US literature documenting the difficulty of operating effective regulatory mechanisms, and the hazard of regulators being 'captured' by those being regulated. The main problem lies in differential access to information between those who are trying to control activities from a distance and those who are actually involved. In economic terms this is an aspect of the 'principal/agent' problem (Vickers and Yarrow, 1988).

In addition, governments are not simple efficiency or utility maximisers, especially at the level of the nation as a whole.[4]

In order to help themselves fulfil their new role, governments need to restructure internally, reducing waste and seeking ways to improve their own capacity to identify problem areas and capitalise on opportunities for collaboration with the private sector, NGOs and farmers' organisations. Unless decision-makers within public sector institutions recognise the rich potential of the environment in which they are acting and the fact that they are no longer the only or even the dominant suppliers, only waste and duplication will result.

Structural ways of enhancing effectiveness and efficiency may be critical. The whole notion of decentralisation within the public sector has been promoted by donors as one sure source of improvement. Apian (1993) details the supposed benefits in the agricultural sector. Decentralised institutions are thought to: better serve the needs of local farmers; reduce central administrative overload; result in faster response to problems at the operational level and improve integration. However, drawing on the example of restructuring in the in Costa Rican research and extension services, he points out that decentralisation may also result in: poor coordination of research; lack of control over research direction; deviation from national development goals and added administrative tasks and linkage requirements. (See Carney (1995) for a fuller discussion of the issues relating to decentralisation, especially of management and supply in agriculture and natural resources.)

Despite strong donor support this strategy cannot be automatically assumed to generate improvements. There is, after all, no guarantee that local decision-making will be any more relevant to farmers' needs than central decision-making; too many other factors come into play. Certainly, though, central institutions must be willing to cede real financial control to decentralised units if improvements are to be forthcoming. However, as Ingham and Kalam (1992) point out, it is frequently only strong governments (such as that in Tanzania) which are prepared to take the risk of decentralising – in which case the decentralisation rarely implies actual autonomy.

Some argue that by reducing the breadth of their commitments governments will naturally increase the depth and efficiency in the target areas in which they remain. However, given the concurrent pressure to cut absolute spending, it is not immediately apparent that target areas will be better resourced. Furthermore, targeting is not a simple process. First, criteria for support must be defined, then questions of degree must be addressed – how far should governments go in their efforts?

---

[4] For example, some argue that they are tools of the dominant classes manipulated into pursuing the narrow interests of this one section of the population (O'Donnell, 1973). Others argue that they pursue their own interests rather than those of the nation as a whole. Thus the political elites which constitute governments seek re-election in the short term and their own aggrandizement in the long term (Migdal, 1988).

Although it is possible to reduce costs by adopting innovative methods in agricultural service provision, especially as levels of rural education improve (for example increased use of mass media and printed matter in extension), other new approaches, especially many participatory development techniques which rely heavily on face to face interaction, are extremely demanding in terms of both time and money (Farrington and Martin, 1988). Resources in most developing countries are very limited and competition to secure them is intense. While rural populations in many developing countries are greater than urban populations, the immediate needs of those in towns are often more visible and arguably sometimes more pressing. This whole issue falls beyond the boundaries of the market and moves into the realms of broad social cost benefit analysis. Such analysis is at best inexact and at worst very manipulable by governments with alternative agendas (see footnote 4).

Finally, whatever level of resources are used in targeting, methods to prevent leakage from target to non-target areas must be found. If they are not, not only will the right people not benefit but the economic environment will also be less attractive to private investors. Demand will fall and economies of scale in operation will be reduced, causing the efficiency of the overall system to suffer.

The overriding conclusion must be, then, that while some solutions will work better than others – and pluralism of supply certainly works better than government or private sector monopolies – there is still much room for improvement in the supply system for agricultural goods and services. In particular there are gaps in the knowledge about the dynamics and actual functioning of new and varied types of systems. For example: how the public sector can best adapt to manage the large numbers of partnerships which it is expected to form with different types of private sector institutions; how participatory approaches to service provision can best be operationalised and cost savings identified; and how the performance of decentralised structures can be effectively monitored and improved upon. Finally, there is the thorny issue of how far governments can go in supporting those sections of the rural population which have little purchasing power without removing all the incentives for these people to seek opportunities for self-help.

In the quest to achieve progress it will be vital not only to consider agriculture and agricultural services but rural livelihoods more broadly. It will also be important to identify effective modes of achieving change. One way of doing this is to work at multiple levels, simultaneously aiming to enhance the effectiveness of national level policy frameworks and to demonstrate the scope for change by investing in concrete projects with local people. The scope for doing this is illustrated in Table 5. De Janvry and Sadoulet (1993) argue that it is only change which is well thought-out, executed for the right reasons and coherent with policy in general which will be effective. Progress certainly seems to be being made in this direction, but there is still some way to go.

Table 5: Scales of intervention

	Agricultural Research	Agricultural Extension	Seed Supply	Rural Finance	Livestock Services	Fertiliser Supply	Agricultural Marketing
Regional or International Level	• Explore options for regional collaboration and technology 'borrowing' • Develop north-south partnerships • Seek donor coordination	• Support cross country learning about reform and non-traditional models (especially private sector options)	• Seek opportunities to increase regional seed trade • Harmonise plant varietal protection legislation	• Support cross country learning about options for and innovations in financial service provision in rural areas	• Support regional disease control efforts	• Cease to provide direct donor shipments	• Assist with analysis and exchange of experience
National Level	• Support links between different parts of NARS • Facilitate inclusive discussion of research priorities • Support involvement of national level farmers' organisations	• Help improve research/extension linkages • Encourage decentralisation of extension responsibility • Develop policy-making capacity for financially sustainable pluralistic system • Develop agricultural curriculum	• Reform regulatory frameworks • Support links between public plant breeders and private suppliers	• Support financial sector reform • Remove barriers to entry for NGOs etc. • Encourage decentralisation of decision-making on credit provision	• Train vets for private practice • Support reform process within government • Improve effectiveness of livestock production research	• Help develop national fertiliser policies and regulation • Help develop private supply network	• Support effective market infrastructure • Monitor effects of reform

| Sub-National or Local Level | • Support local level priority setting with stakeholders
• Explore options for research funds
• Help develop demand side for research | • Understand local knowledge systems and uptake pathways
• Provide training in participatory methods
• Provide funds for research/extension partnerships | • Understand farmers' seed needs
• Explore options for safeguarding genetic diversity
• Support local seed enterprises | • Understand local credit systems and information sources
• Support innovation in credit schemes (and monitor) | • Train paravets
• Support membership organisations
• Support local marketing systems | • Provide targeted subsidies
• Help fine tune fertiliser recommendations through on-farm research | • Provide direct support to private sector, private sector associations and marketing groups
• Support training for trade |

Bibliography

Aguirre, F. and Namdar-Irani, M. (1992) *Complementarities and Tensions in NGO-State Relations in Agricultural Development: The Trajectory of Agraria (Chile)*. Agricultural Research and Extension Network Paper No. 32. London: Overseas Development Institute.

Ahmed, R. and Hossain, M. (1990) *Development Impact of Rural Infrastructure in Bangladesh*, Research Report 83. International Food Policy Research Institute in collaboration with the Bangladesh Institute of Development Studies, October 1990.

Alex, G. (1997) *Lessons from Recent Experiences with Research Investment Strategies*. Paper presented at Workshop on New Investment Strategies for Agriculture and Natural Resources Research. London October 1997.

Alston, J.M. and Pardey, P.G. (1996) *Making Science Pay: The Economics of Agricultural R&D Policy*. Washington, D.C.: AEI Press.

Amanor, K. and Farrington, J. (1991) 'NGOs and Agricultural Technology Development' in W.M. Rivera and D.J. Gustafson (eds) *Agricultural Extension: Worldwide Institutional Evolution and Forces for Change*. Amsterdam: Elsevier.

Ameur, C. (1994) *Agricultural Extension: A Step Beyond the Next Step*. World Bank Technical Paper No. 247. Washington, D.C.: World Bank Publications.

Anderson, J.R. (ed.) (1994) *Agricultural Technology: Policy Issues for the International Community*. Wallingford: CAB International.

Anderson, J.R. and de Haan, C. (eds) *Public and Private Roles in Agricultural Development: Proceedings of the Twelfth Agricultural Sector Symposium*. Washington, D.C.: World Bank Publications.

Antholt, C.H. (1994) Getting Ready for the Twenty-First Century: Technical Change and Institutional Modernization in Agriculture. World Bank Technical Paper No. 217. Washington, D.C.: World Bank Publications.

Apian, T. (1993) *Partners in Agricultural Technology: Linking Research and Technology Transfer to Serve Farmers*. ISNAR Research Report No. 1. The Hague: ISNAR.

Ashby, J.A. and Sperling, L. (1994) *Institutionalising Participatory, Client-Driven Research and Technology Development in Agriculture*. ODI Agricultural Research and Extension Network Paper No. 49. London: Overseas Development Institute.

Asian Productivity Organisation (1992) 'Summary of Findings' in *Mobilization of Rural Savings in Asia and The Pacific*. Report of an APO Symposium held in Tokyo 27 November to 4 December 1990. Tokyo: Asian Productivity Organisation.

Auroi, C. (ed.) (1992) *The Role of the State in Development Processes*. EADI Book Series No. 15. London: Frank Cass.

Bates, R.H. (1981) *Markets and States in Tropical Africa: The Political Basis of Agricultural Policies*. Berkeley: University of California Press.

Bates, R.H. (1989) 'The Reality of Structural Adjustment: A Sceptical Appraisal' in S. Commander (ed) *Structural Adjustment and Agriculture: Theory and Practice in Africa and Latin America*. London: Overseas Development Institute.

Bebbington, A., Quisbert, J. and Trujillo, G. (1996) *Technology and Rural Development Strategies in a Base Economic Organisation: 'El Ceibo' Ltd Federation of*

Cooperatives. Agricultural Research and Extension Network Paper No. 62. London: Overseas Development Institute.

Bebbington A. and Thiele, G. (1993) *Non-Governmental Organizations and the State in Latin America: Rethinking Roles in Sustainable Agricultural Development.* London: Routledge.

Bebbington, A.J. et al. (1993) *Rural Peoples' Knowledge, Farmer Organisations and Regional Development: Implications for Agricultural Research and Development.* ODI Agricultural Research and Extension Network Paper No. 41. London: Overseas Development Institute.

Bebbington, A.J. and Farrington, J. (1992) 'Private Voluntary Initiatives: Enhancing the Public Sector's Capacity to Respond to Nongovernmental Organization Needs' in J.R. Anderson and C. de Haan (eds) *Public and Private Roles in Agricultural Development: Proceedings of the Twelfth Agricultural Sector Symposium.* Washington, D.C.: World Bank Publications.

Bebbington, A.J., Merrill-Sands, D. and Farrington, J. (1994) *Farmer and Community Organisations in Agricultural Research and Extension: Functions, Impacts and Questions.* ODI Agricultural Research and Extension Network Paper No. 47. London: Overseas Development Institute.

Berdegué, J.A. (1994) 'Chile's Privatized Extension System: 17 Years of Experience'. Paper presented at the International Symposium on Systems-Based Approaches to Agricultural and Rural Development, Montpellier, France, 21–25 November 1994.

Berdegué, J.A. (1997) 'Organisation of Agricultural Extension and Advisory Services for Small Farmers in Selected Latin American Countries'. Paper presented at Tune Conference on *Technology Development and Transfer.* April, 1997, Tune, Denmark.

Beynon, J. & Duncan, A. (1996) *Financing of Agricultural Research and Extension for Smallholder Farmers in Sub-Saharan Africa: Summary Report and Operational Guidelines.* Oxford: Food Studies Group.

Beynon, J. and Mbogoh, S. (1996) *Financing of Agricultural Research and Extension for Smallholder Farmers in sub-Saharan Africa: the Case of Agricultural Research in Kenya.* Mimeo. Oxford: Food Studies Group.

Bingen, R.J. (1994) 'Agricultural Development Policy and Grassroots Democracy in Mali: The Emergence of Mali's Farmer Movement'. *African Rural and Urban Studies* 1: No 1 1994. Michigan State University.

Blench, R.M. (1998) *Fragments and Sentiments: Why is the 'Community' the focus of Development? - check with DC that this is the right one.* Agricultural Research and Extension Network Paper 81a. London: Overseas Development Institute.

Blum, A. (1991) 'An Improved Agricultural Knowledge System: The Israeli Experience with Regional Research and Development Authorities' in W.M. Rivera and D.J. Gustafson (eds) *Agricultural Extension: Worldwide Institutional Evolution and Forces for Change.* Amsterdam: Elsevier.

Bratton, M. and Bingen, R.J. (1994) 'Farmer Organization and Agricultural Policy in Africa – Introduction'. *African Rural and Urban Studies* 1: No 1 1994. Michigan State University.

Brenner, C. (1991) *Biotechnology and Developing Country Agriculture: The Case of Maize.* Paris: OECD.

Byerlee, D. (1996) 'Modern Varieties, Productivity, and Sustainability: Recent Experience and Emerging Challenges'. *World Development,* 24(4), pp. 697–718.

Carney, D. (1995) *Management and Supply in Agriculture and Natural Resources: in Decentralisation the Answer?* ODI Natural Perspective Paper No 4. London: Overseas Development Institute.

Carney, D. (1996) 'Formal Farmers' Organisations in the Agricultural Technology System: Current Roles and Future Challenges.' ODI Natural Resources Perspective Paper No 14. London: Overseas Development Institute.

Carney, D. (1997) 'Alternative Systems for Financing Agricultural Technology Research and Development in Uganda, Tanzania and Kenya.' Report to BDDEA, Department for International Development. Overseas Development Institute.

Carney, D. and Farrington, J. (1998) *Natural Resources Management and Institutional Change.* London: Routledge (in press).

Carney, D. and Farrington, J. (1998) Papers presented at workshop on *New Investment Strategies for Agricultural and Natural Resources Research.* London, October 1997.

CECAT/RCRE (1996) *Farmers' Technical Association in China.* Beijing: CECAT/RCRE.

Christoplos, I. (1996) 'Rural Extension: Guidelines for Sida Support.' Paper presented to the *Second In formal Consultation on International Support to Agricultural Extension Systems in Africa,* Rome, Italy 8–9 October 1996.Cleaver, K.M. (1993) *A Strategy to Develop Agriculture in Sub-Saharan Africa and a Focus for the World Bank.* Washington, D.C.: World Bank Publications.

Collion, M-H. (1994) 'Farmers and Researchers: The Road to Partnership in Mali', paper presented at ODI/ISNAR Practitioner's Workshop on Research and Farmers' Organisations: Prospects for Partnership, The Hague, June 1994.

Collion, M.-H. and Rondot, P. (1998) *Partnerships between Agricultural Services Institutions and Producers' Organisations: Myth or Reality.* Agricultural Research and Extension Network Paper No. 80. London: Overseas Development Institute.

Commander, S. (ed.) (1989) *Structural Adjustment and Agriculture: Theory and Practice in Africa and Latin America.* London: Overseas Development Institute.

Compton, J. (1997) Managing Applied Research: Experiences from a Post-Harvest Pest Control Project in Ghana. Agricultural Research and Extension Network Paper No. 74a London: Overseas Development Institute.

Coutu, A. and O'Donnell, J. (1991) 'Agricultural Development Foundations: A Private Sector Innovation in Improving Agricultural Technology Systems' in W.M. Rivera and D.J. Gustafson (eds) *Agricultural Extension: Worldwide Institutional Evolution and Forces for Change.* Amsterdam: Elsevier.

Cromwell, E. (1992) *The Impact of Economic Reform on the Performance of the Seed Sector in Eastern and Southern Africa.* OECD Development Centre Technical Paper No. 68. Paris: OECD.

Cromwell, E. and Wiggins, S. (1993) *Sowing Beyond the State: NGOs and Seed Supply in Developing Countries.* London: Overseas Development Institute.

Crosson, P. & Anderson, J.R. (1994) 'Demand and Supply: Trends in Global Agriculture'. *Food Policy,* 19(2), pp. 105–119.

Cuevas, C.E. (1988) 'Savings and Loans Cooperatives in Rural Areas of Developing Countries: Recent Performance and Potential'. *Savings and Development* No.1 1988 XII: 5–15.

Dalrymple, D.G. and Srivastava, J.P. (1994) 'Transfer of Plant Cultivars: Seeds, Sectors and Society' in J.R. Anderson (ed.) *Agricultural Technology: Policy Issues for the International Community*. Wallingford: CAB International.

de Coninck, J. and Tinguiri, K.L. (1992) 'Niger' in A. Duncan and J. Howell (eds) *Structural Adjustment and the African Farmer*. London: Overseas Development Institute.

de Janvry, A. and Sadoulet, E. (1993) 'Market, State and Civil Organizations in Latin America Beyond the Debt Crisis: The Context for Rural Development'. *World Development* 21(4): 659–674.

de Kadt, E., Mars, Z. and White, G. (1992) 'State and Development into the 1990s: the Issues for Researchers' in C. Auroi (ed.) *The Role of the State in Development Processes*. EADI Book Series No. 15. Frank Cass: London.

Duncan, A. and Howell, J. (eds) (1992) *Structural Adjustment and the African Farmer*. London: Overseas Development Institute.

Egaitsu, F. (1992) 'Credit First? or Deposit First? Answers to Two Major Questions Based on the Country Report' in *Mobilization of Rural Savings in Asia and The Pacific* Report of an APO Symposium held in Tokyo 27 November to 4 December 1990. Tokyo: Asian Productivity Organisation.

Ellis, F. (1993) 'Private Trade and Public Role in Staple Food Marketing: The Case of Rice in Indonesia'. *Food Policy*, 18(5), October 1993: 428–438.

Esman, M.J. and Uphoff, N.T. (1984) *Local Organizations: Intermediaries in Rural Development*. Ithaca, NY: Cornell University Press.

Evenson, R. and David, C. (1993) *Adjustment and Technology: The Case of Rice*. Paris: OECD.

Eyzaguirre, P. (1996) *Agricultural and Environmental Research in Small Countries: Innovative Approaches to Strategic Planning*. Chichester, UK: John Wiley and Sons.

FAO (1993) 'Quality Declared Seed.' *FAO Plant Production and Protection Paper 117*. Rome.

Farrington, J. (1994) *Public Sector Agricultural Extension: Is there Life after Structural Adjustment?* ODI Natural Resource Perspectives, Number 2. London: Overseas Development Institute.

Farrington, J. and Bebbington, A.. (1993) *Reluctant Partners? Non-Governmental Organizations, the State and Sustainable Agricultural Development*. London: Routledge.

Farrington, J. and Martin, A. (1988) *Farmer Participation in Agricultural Research: A Review of Concepts and Practices*. ODI Agricultural Administration Unit Occasional Paper Number 9. London: Overseas Development Institute.

Fontaine, J-M. and Sindzingre, A. (1991) *Macro-Micro Linkages: Structural Adjustment and Fertilizer Policy in Sub-Saharan Africa*. OECD Development Centre Technical Paper No. 49. Paris: OECD.

Grandin, B., Thampy, R. and Young, J. (1991) *Village Animal Healthcare: A Community-based Approach to Livestock Development in Kenya*. London: Intermediate Technology Publications.

Grobman, A. (1992) 'Fostering a Fledgling Seed Industry' in J.R. Anderson and C. de Haan (eds) *Public and Private Roles in Agricultural Development: Proceedings of the Twelfth Agricultural Sector Symposium*. Washington, D.C.: World Bank Publications.

Gros, J.-G. (1994) 'Of Cattle, Farmers, Veterinarians and the World Bank: the Political Economy of Veterinary Services Privatization in Cameroun'. *Public Administration and Development*, 14(1): 37–51.

Gubbels, P. (1994) *The Role of Peasant Farmer Organization in Transforming Agricultural Research and Extension Practice in West Africa*. Paper given to the CTA workshop on Agricultural Extension in Africa. Yaounde, Cameroon. January 1994.

Hagmann, J., Chuma, E., Connolly, M. and Murwira, K. (1998) *Client-driven Change and Institutional Reform in Agricultural Extension: An Action Learning Experience from Zimbabwe*. Agricultural Research and Extension Network Paper No. 78. London: Overseas Development Institute.

Healy, K. (1987) 'From Field to Factory: Vertical Integration in Bolivia'. *Grassroots Development*, 11(2): 2–11.

Hercus, J. (1991) 'The Commercialization of Government Agricultural Extension Service in New Zealand' in W.M. Rivera and D.J. Gustafson (eds) *Agricultural Extension: Worldwide Institutional Evolution and Forces for Change*. Amsterdam: Elsevier.

Hewitt, A. (1992) 'Madagascar' in A. Duncan and J. Howell (eds) *Structural Adjustment and the African Farmer*. London: Overseas Development Institute.

Hobbs, S.H. and Taylor, T.A. (1987) *Agricultural Research in the Private Sector in Africa*. ISNAR Working Paper No. 8. The Hague: ISNAR.

Hubbard, M. and Smith, M. (1996) *The Role of Government in Adjusting Economies*. Agricultural Marketing Sector Review Paper 6. Birmingham: Development Administration Group, University of Birmingham.

Hulme, D. (1991) 'Agricultural Extension Services as Machines: The Impact of the T&V Approach' in W.M. Rivera and D.J. Gustafson (eds) *Agricultural Extension: Worldwide Institutional Evolution and Forces for Change*. Amsterdam: Elsevier.

Hulme, D. and P. Mosely (1996) *Finance Against Poverty*. London: Routledge.

Hunting Technical Services Ltd. (1994) *Mid Term Report: Bangladesh Agricultural Support Services Project*.

Husain, I. and Faruqee, R. (eds) (1994) *Adjustment in Africa: Lessons from Country Case Studies*. Washington, D.C.: World Bank Publications.

Ingham, B. and Kalam, A.K.M. (1992) 'Decentralisation and Development: Theory and Evidence from Bangladesh'. *Public Administration and Development*, Vol 12: 373–385.

Ingram, P. (1992) 'The United Kingdom Experience in the Privatization of Extension' in J.R. Anderson and C. de Haan (eds) *Public and Private Roles in Agricultural Development: Proceedings of the Twelfth Agricultural Sector Symposium*. Washington, D.C.: World Bank Publications.

Isa, M.M. (1992) 'Credit and Savings: The Grameen Bank's Experience' in *Mobilization of Rural Savings in Asia and The Pacific* Report of an APO Symposium held in Tokyo 27 November to 4 December 1990. Tokyo: Asian Productivity Organisation.

Jaeger, W.K. (1992) *The Effects of Economic Policies on African Agriculture*. World Bank Discussion Paper 147. Washington, D.C.: World Bank Publications.

Jain, P.J. (1992) 'Managing Credit for the Rural Poor: Lessons from the Grameen Bank' *World Development* Vol. 24. No 1. pp.79–89.

James, A. and Upton, M. (1995) *Cost Recovery for Veterinary Services*. University of Reading.
Jarvis, L.S. (1994) 'Changing Private and Public Roles in Technological Development: Lessons from the Chilean Fruit Sector' in J.R. Anderson (ed.) *Agricultural Technology: Policy Issues for the International Community*. Wallingford: CAB International.
Kafo Jiginiew Rapport d'Exercice (Annual Report and Accounts) (1994). Fédération des Caisses Mutuelles d'Epargne et de Credit Mali-Sud.
Kaimowitz, D. (ed.) (1990) *Making the Link: Agricultural Research and Technology Transfer in Developing Countries*. Boulder, Colorado: Westview.
Kelly, V. A. (1988) *Farmers' Demand for Fertilizer in the Context of Senegal's New Agricultural Policy: A Study of Factors Influencing Farmers' Fertilizer Purchasing Decisions*. MSU International Development Papers, Reprint No. 19. East Lansing, Michigan: MSU.
Khan, M. et al. (1991) *NGO Interactions with the Public Sector: The Experience of Proshika's Livestock and Social Forestry Programme*. Agricultural Research and Extension Network Paper No. 26. London: Overseas Development Institute.
Klitgaard, R. (1991) *Adjusting to Reality: Beyond "State Versus Marker" in Economic Development*. San Francisco: ICS Press.
Korten, D.C. (1980) 'Community Organization in Rural Development: A Learning Process Approach'. *Public Administration Review*, September/October 1980.
Larson, B.A. & Frisvold, G.B. (1996) 'Fertilizers to Support Agricultural Development in Sub-Saharan Africa: What is Needed and Why'. *Food Policy*, 21(6), pp. 509–525.
Leonard, D. (1985) *The Supply of Veterinary Services*. Harvard Institute for International Development, Discussion Paper 191. Cambridge, Mass.: HIID.
Leonard, D. (1993) 'Structural Reform of the Veterinary Profession in Africa and the New Institutional Economics'. *Development and Change* 24: 227–267.
Lewa, P.M. (1995) 'Kenya's Cereal Sector Reform Programme: Managing the Politics of Reform', Paper presented at University of Birmingham workshop on The Changing Public Role in Services to Agriculture, 24th April, 1995.
Long, N. and Long, A. (eds) (1992) *Battlefields of Knowledge: The interlocking of theory and practice in social development Research*. London: Routledge
Maalouf, W.D., Contado, T.E. and Adhikarya, R. (1991) 'Extension Coverage and Resource Problems: The Need for Public-Private Cooperation' in W.M. Rivera and D.J. Gustafson (eds) *Agricultural Extension: Worldwide Institutional Evolution and Forces for Change*. Amsterdam: Elsevier.
Mans, D. (1994) 'Tanzania: resolute action' in I. Husain and R. Faruqee (eds) *Adjustment in Africa: Lessons from Country Case Studies*. Washington, D.C.: World Bank Publications.
Marsden, K. (1990) *African Entrepreneurs: Pioneers of Development*. IFC Discussion Paper No. 9. Washington, D.C.: World Bank Publications.
Merrill-Sands, D. and Kaimowitz, D. (1991) *The Technology Triangle: Linking farmers technology transfer agents and agricultural researchers*. The Hague: ISNAR.
Merrill-Sands, D. and Collion, M.-H. (1993) 'Making the Farmer's Voice Count in Agricultural Research'. *Quarterly Journal of International Agriculture* 32(3): 260–279.

Migdal, J. (1988) *Strong Societies and Weak States: State-Society Relations and State Capabilities in the Third World.* Princeton, NJ: Princeton University Press.

Mitti, G., Drinkwater, M. and Kalonge, S. (1997) *Experimenting with Agricultural Extension in Zambia: CARE' Livingstone Food Security Project.* Agricultural Research and Extension Network Paper 77. London: Overseas Development Institute.

Mosse, D. (With the KRIBP team) (1996) *Local Institutions and Farming Systems Development: Thoughts from and Project in Tribal Western India.* Agricultural Research and Extension Network Paper 64. London: Overseas Development Institute.

Nugent, J.B. (1993) 'Between State, Market and Households: A Neoinstitutional Analysis of Local organisations and Institutions'. *World Development* 21(4): 623–632.

Nuitjen, M. (1992) 'Local Organization as Organizing Practices: Rethinking Rural Institutions' in Long and Long (eds) *Battlefields of Knowledge.* London: Routledge.

Nunberg, B. and Nellis, J. (1990) *Civil Service Reform and the World Bank.* World Bank WPS 422. Washington, D.C.: World Bank Publications.

ODA (1994) *Private Sector Development.* Technical Note No. 11. London: ODA.

Odeyemi, I.A.O. (1994) *Modelling Area Viability for Private Veterinary Practices in Africa: A Conceptual Approach.* Edinburgh: Centre for Tropical Veterinary Medicine.

O'Donnell, G. (1973) *Modernization and Bureaucratic-Authoritarianism.* Berkeley: University of California Press.

Okali, C., Sumberg, J. and Farrington, J. (1994) *Farmer Participatory Research.* London: Intermediate Technology.

Olsen, F.W. (1996) 'Farmer Managed Agricultural Extension.' Paper presented at the second informal consultation on *International Support to Agricultural Extension Systems in Africa.* Rome, October 1996.

Overseas Development Institute (1986) *Privatisation: The Developing Country Experience.* Briefing Paper, September 1986. London: Overseas Development Institute.

Overseas Development Institute (1993) *Patenting Plants: The Implications for Developing Countries.* Briefing Paper, November 1993. London: Overseas Development Institute.

Overseas Development Institute (1994) *The CGIAR: What Future for International Agricultural Research?* Briefing Paper, September 1993. London: Overseas Development Institute.

Padmanabhan, K.P. (1988) *Rural Credit: Lessons for Rural Bankers and Policy Makers.* London: Intermediate Technology Publications.

Pardey, P.G., Roseboom, J. and Anderson, J.R. (eds) (1991) *Agricultural Research Policy: International Quantitative Perspectives.* Cambridge: CUP.

Parish, D.H. (1992) 'New Technologies in Soil Fertility Maintenance: Private Sector Contribution' in J.R. Anderson and C. de Haan (eds) *Public and Private Roles in Agricultural Development: Proceedings of the Twelfth Agricultural Sector Symposium.* Washington, D.C.: World Bank Publications.

Pearce, R. (1992) 'Ghana' in A. Duncan and J. Howell (eds) *Structural Adjustment and the African Farmer.* London: Overseas Development Institute.

Pijnenburg, B. (1998) *Limits to Farmer Participation.* Agricultural Research and Extension Network Newsletter 37. London: Overseas Development Institute.

Piñeiro, M. (1986) *The Development of the Private Sector in Agricultural Research: Implications for Public Research Institutions.* ISNAR Proagro Paper No. 10. The Hague: ISNAR.

Poulton, C., Dorward, A. and Kydd, J. (1997) *Interlocking Transactions: Market Alternatives for RNR Services.* Final report to the Department for International Development. Ashford: Wye College.

Pray, C.E. and Echeverria, R.G. (1991) 'Private Sector Agricultural Research in Less Developed Countries' in Pardey et al. (eds) *Agricultural Research Policy: International Quantitative Perspectives.* Cambridge: CUP.

Pray, C.E. and Echeverria, R.G. (1990) 'Private Sector Agricultural Research and Technology Transfer Links in Developing Countries' in Kaimowitz (ed.) *Making the Link: Agricultural Research and Technology Transfer in Developing Countries.* Boulder: Westview.

Purcell, D.L. and Anderson, J.R. (1997) *Agricultural Extension and Research: Achievements and Problems in National Systems.* World Bank Operations Evaluation Study. Washington, D.C.: World Bank.

Quiroz, J.A. & Valdes, A. (1995) 'Agricultural Diversification and Policy Reform'. *Food Policy*, 20(3), pp. 245–255.

Rivera, W.M. and Gustafson, D.J. (1991) (eds) *Agricultural Extension: Worldwide Institutional Evolution and Forces for Change.* Amsterdam: Elsevier.

Rogaly, B. (1997) *The Role of Co-operatives and Self-Help Organisations in Financial Services.* DFID Desk Review. Norwich: University of East Anglia.

Röling, N. (1991) 'The Development of the Concept of Agricultural Knowledge Information Systems: Implications for Extension' in W.M. Rivera and D.J. Gustafson (eds) *Agricultural Extension: Worldwide Institutional Evolution and Forces for Change.* Amsterdam: Elsevier.

Röling, N. (1990) 'The Agricultural Research-Technology Transfer Interface: A Knowledge Systems Perspective' in Kaimowitz (ed.) *Making the Link: Agricultural Research and Technology Transfer in Developing Countries.* Boulder: Westview.

Schiff, M. and Valdés, A. (1992) *The Plundering of Agriculture in Developing Countries.* Washington, D.C.: World Bank Publications.

Schwartz, L.A. (1994) *The Role of the Private Sector in Agricultural Extension: Economic Analysis and Case Studies.* Agricultural Research and Extension Network Paper No. 48. London: Overseas Development Institute.

Shepherd, A. (1989) 'Approaches to the Privatization of Fertilizer marketing in Africa'. *Food Policy*, 14(2), May 1989: 143–154.

Sims, H. and Leonard, D. (1990) 'The Political Economy of the Development and Transfer of Agricultural Technologies Perspective' in Kaimowitz (ed.) *Making the Link: Agricultural Research and Technology Transfer in Developing Countries.* Boulder: Westview.

Smith, L. D. and Thomson, A. M. (1991) *The Role of Public and Private Agents in the Food and Agriculture Sectors of Developing Countries.* FAO, Economic and Social Development Paper 105. Rome: FAO.

Sperling, L. Scheidegger, U. and Buruchara, R. (1996) *Designing Seed Systems with Small Farmers: Principles Derived from Bean Research in the Great Lakes Region of Africa*. Agricultural Research and Extension Network Paper No. 60. London: Overseas Development Institute.

Srivastava, J.P. and Jaffee, S. (1993) *Best Practices for Moving Seed Technology: New Approaches to Doing Business*. World Bank Technical Paper No. 213. Washington, D.C.: World Bank Publications.

Streeten, P. (1996) 'Globalisation and Competitiveness: What are the Implications for Development Thinking and Practice?'. Main Paper presented at the *Development Thinking and Practice Conference*, Washington D.C., 3–5 September 1996.

Stringfellow, R., Coulter, J., Lucey, T., McKone, C. and Hussain, A. (1997) 'Improving the Access of Smallholders to Agricultural Services in Sub-Saharan Africa: Farmer Cooperation and the Role of the Donor Community.' *Natural Resource Perspectives No. 20*. London: Overseas Development Institute.

Sumberg, J. and Okali, C. (1997) *Farmers' Experiments: Creating Local Knowledge*. Boulder, Co.: Lynne Reiner.

Sutherland, A.J., Irungu, J.W., Kang'ara, J., Muthamia, J. and Ouma J. (1998) *Tackling Household Food Security through Adaptive Research: Lessons from the Dryland Applied Research and Extension Project, Kenya*. Agricultural Research and Extension Network Paper No. 79. London: Overseas Development Institute.

Suresh, P., Bahl, D.K. and Mruthyunjaya (1993) 'Government Interventions in Foodgrain Markets: The Case of India'. *Food Policy*, 18(5), October 1993: 414–427.

Swamy, G. (1994) 'Kenya: patchy, intermittent commitment' in I. Husain and R. Faruqee (eds) *Adjustment in Africa: Lessons from Country Case Studies*. Washington, D.C.: World Bank Publications.

Tendler, J. *Good Government in the Tropics*. Baltimore and London: John Hopkins University Press.

Thirtle, C. and Echeverria, R.G. (1994) 'Privatization and the Roles of Public and Private Institutions in Agricultural Research in Sub-Saharan Africa'. *Food Policy* 19(1): 31–44.

Thomson, A.M. (1991) *Institutional changes in agricultural product and input markets and their impact on agricultural performance*. FAO, Economic and Social Development Paper 98. Rome: FAO.

Timmer, C.P. (1992) 'Agriculture and Economic Development Revisited'. *Agricultural Systems*, 38(6), pp.21–58.

Toye, J. 'Is there a New Political Economy of Development?' in C. Colclough and J. Manor (eds) *States or Markets? Neo-liberalism and the Development Policy Debate*. Oxford: Clarendon Press.

Tripp, R. (1991) *Planned Change in Farming Systems: Progress in On-Farm Research*. Chichester: John Wiley and Sons.

Tripp, R., Louwaars, N., van der Burg, W.J., Virk, D.S. and Witcombe, J.R. (1997) *Alternatives for Seed Regulatory Reform: An Analysis of Variety Testing, Variety Regulation and Seed Quality Control*. ODI Agricultural Research and Extension Network Paper No. 69. London: Overseas Development Institute.

Umali, D. L., Feder, G. and de Haan, C. (1992) *The Balance between Public and Private Sector Activities in the Delivery of Livestock Services*. World Bank Discussion Paper No. 163. Washington, D.C.: World Bank Publications.

Umali, D. L. and Schwartz, L. (1994) *Public and Private Agricultural Extension: Beyond Traditional Frontiers*. World Bank Discussion Paper No. 236. Washington, D.C.: World Bank Publications.

USAID (1996) *Endowments in Africa: A Discussion of Issues for Using Alternative Financing Mechanisms to Support Agricultural and Natural Resources Management Programs*. Technical Paper no. 24 (Office of Sustainable Development, Bureau for Africa). Washington D.C.: USAID.

Venkatesan, V. and Schwartz, L. (1992) *Agricultural Services Initiative*. Agriculture and Rural Development Series No.4, based upon World Bank Workshop held at Lilongwe in February 1991. Washington, D.C.: World Bank Publications.

Vickers, J. and Yarrow, G. (1988) *Privatization: An Economic Analysis*. Cambridge, Ma.: MIT Press.

Vogel, R.C. (1992) 'Successful Rural Savings Mobilization: The Incentives Required and the Discipline They Provide' in *Mobilization of Rural Savings in Asia and The Pacific* Report of an APO Symposium held in Tokyo 27 November to 4 December 1990. Tokyo: Asian Productivity Organisation.

Wilson, M. (1991) 'Reducing the Costs of Public Extension Services: Initiatives in Latin America' in W.M. Rivera and D.J. Gustafson (eds) *Agricultural Extension: Worldwide Institutional Evolution and Forces for Change*. Amsterdam: Elsevier.

World Bank, Agriculture and Natural Resources Department (1993) *Agricultural Sector Review*. Washington, D.C.: World Bank Publications.

World Bank (1981) *Accelerated Development in Sub-Saharan Africa: An Agenda for Action*. Washington, D.C.: World Bank Publications.

World Bank (1994a) Adjustment in Africa: Reforms, Results and the Road Ahead. New York: Oxford University Press.

World Bank Operations Evaluation Department (1994b) *Agricultural Extension: Lessons from Completed Projects*. Washington, D.C.: World Bank Publications.

World Bank (1994c) *World Development Report 1994: Infrastructure for Development*. New York: Oxford University Press.

Yaron, J. (1992a) 'Rural Finance in Developing Countries' in J.R. Anderson and C. de Haan (eds) *Public and Private Roles in Agricultural Development: Proceedings of the Twelfth Agricultural Sector Symposium*. Washington, D.C.: World Bank Publications.

Yaron, J. (1992b) *Rural Finance in Developing Countries*. World Bank WPS 875. Washington D.C.: World Bank Publications.